THE INTERNATIONAL PSYCHO-ANALYTICAL LIBRARY

EDITED BY JOHN SUTHERLAND, M.D., PH.D.

No. 60

THE FAMILY AND
HUMAN ADAPTATION

THREE LECTURES

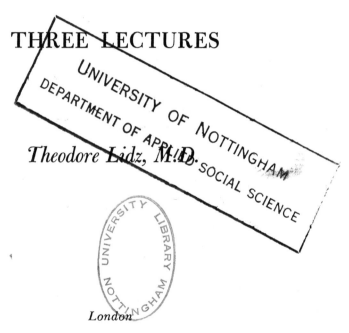

Theodore Lidz, M.D.

London

THE HOGARTH PRESS
AND THE INSTITUTE OF PSYCHO-ANALYSIS

1964

PUBLISHED BY

THE HOGARTH PRESS LTD.

Copyright 1963
International Universities Press, Inc.

Presented as the

Mona Bronfman Sheckman Lectures in Social Psychiatry
at Tulane University, New Orleans, Louisiana
February 23 and 24, 1961

(

PRINTED IN THE UNITED STATES OF AMERICA

THE INTERNATIONAL
PSYCHO-ANALYTICAL LIBRARY
No. 60

Contents

Acknowledgments

DURING THE past ten years I have been working in constant collaboration with Dr. Stephen Fleck and Miss Alice Cornelison on studies pertaining to schizophrenia. Many of the ideas expressed, particularly in the second lecture, emerged from our studies and are theirs as much as mine, but I accept responsibility for the concepts as presented in these lectures. I wish to express my indebtedness to them and my appreciation for all they have contributed.

A number of others have participated in carrying out various parts of our studies and have made significant contributions to them—Dr. Dorothy Terry, Dr. Beulah Parker, Dr. Daniel Freedman, Mrs. Sarah Schafer, Dr. Ezra Vogel, Mrs. Eleanor Kay, Dr. Bernice Rosman, and Dr. Cynthia Wild. I wish to thank our secretaries Miss Hope Mag and Mrs. Catherine Molloy for their devotion to the project, and Mrs. Harriette Borsuch who patiently typed, retyped, and tactfully corrected many versions of these lectures.

The investigations of families containing schizophrenic and delinquent offspring were supported by the National Institute of Mental Health and the Social Research Foundation. I also wish to thank the Commonwealth Fund for its support of a sabbatical leave as these lectures reflect concepts concerning personality development formulated during that year.

[1]

Introduction

THESE LECTURES explore the critical role of the family in human adaptation and integration. Man can grow up and live in widely divergent environments because each society possesses techniques that extend his biological adaptive capacities, and indoctrinates its members into the institutions, evolved over millennia, for coping with the environment and for living together. The family has, everywhere, been the society's primary agency in providing for the child's biological needs and simultaneously directing his development into an integrated person capable of living in a society and maintaining and transmitting its culture. The family is an essential derivative of man's biological make-up and, at the same time, the basic social institution that permits his survival by augmenting his inborn adaptive capacities. Because the family must provide for basic needs common to all mankind, it has similar functions and similarities of structure everywhere. Yet, within these limits, the family can and must vary widely to fit into, and assure the continuity of, the very divergent societies of which it is a subsystem. Can we define the fundamentals that must be maintained within these variations? Without

[3]

more explicit information than we now possess concerning the functions of the family and how the family functions, a hiatus exists that impedes our understanding of personality development on the one hand, and our grasp of the modifiability and the process of modification of social institutions on the other. In these lectures, I explore the thesis that through comprehension of the family's role in mediating between man's two endowments—his genetic inheritance and his cultural heritage—a proper fusion of the biological and cultural orientations to the study of human behavior and its aberrations can be achieved which will eliminate many of our current dualisms, vagaries, and factional quarrels.

In these lectures, which were presented to an audience of psychiatrists, anthropologists, psychologists, and sociologists at Tulane University, I sought to discuss topics of equal moment to all of these disciplines. The specific topics, however, were selected out of my own need to pursue a few critical questions that had arisen during an intensive study of a series of patients and their families. The audience was, in effect, asked to accompany me in my quest. I believe that the questions opened the way for some new insights into problems of human adaptation and thereby raised numerous other questions that remain unanswered.

Although the concepts considered in these pages arose from studies of families with schizophrenic offspring, they are not primarily concerned with schizophrenia, but with problems of adaptation and integration. Nevertheless, they may form a prolegomena to a general theory of schizophrenia. Schizophrenia, whatever else may be involved, can be defined as a gross failure to achieve or maintain ego integration. It is a failure of the adaptive capacities. Traditionally, investigators had considered the failure to reflect some unknown type of impairment of brain function, primarily because of the disorders of thought and language that are characteristic of schizophrenia. However, these distortions of thought are very different from those caused by any known type of brain dysfunction. A grasp of the complexities of the acquisition of language and logic by the child suggested the potentiality that schizophrenic patients received a faulty and confused grounding in linguistic meanings, as well as in other instrumental techniques, that both limited their adaptive capacities and permitted them to escape from insoluble conflict or irreconcilable contradictions by abandoning the meaning system of their culture. As children obtain their fundamental training in meanings and logic within the family, and as irreconcilable conflicts also usually have their roots within the family, it appeared essential to scrutinize the family environments in which schizophrenic patients grew up. Investigations have now revealed that they had always been raised in seriously disturbed families which almost always contained at least one unusually disturbed parent.

The focusing of attention upon the nurturant family environment with which the patient's personality interacted as it unfolded, and which the child assimilated as he developed, has proven rewarding. Various characteristics of the families of schizophrenic patients that may have pertinence to the genesis of schizophrenia have been delineated. However, as virtually every area of interaction in these families is faulty in some respect, the question arises if something may not be fundamentally amiss in the integration of these families, or if something essential to the proper development of their children may not be lacking. The study of schizophrenia has thus directed interest to the study of the structure and functions of the family and how it subserves human adaptation.

Pathology is often the highroad to the understanding of physiology. The disruptions of human adaptation help reveal the complexity of the process and the functions of the various components. Disorders of various endocrine glands first provided understanding of their functions and their interrelationships; damage that disrupted the integrated functioning of the brain opened the way for the localization of brain functions. Similarly, schizophrenia provides opportunity to scrutinize some fundamental problems of human integration that are not uncovered in lesser disturbances. Although unproven, the hypothesis that schizophrenia is a type of maladaptation and malintegration due to deficiencies in acquiring instrumental techniques and ego structuring rather than caused by some process that disrupts the integrative capacities of the brain has become tenable. According to this hypothesis, schizophrenia can become a means of gaining new insights into the development of the uniquely human adaptive capacities, and the study of the families in which schizophrenic patients grew up can provide new insights into the family as an essential human institution.

[6]

The importance of the family to the child's personality development has, of course, been recognized by all dynamic theories of personality. Psychoanalysis, in particular, despite a period during which innate causes of libidinal fixation were emphasized, has directed attention to maternal nurturant behavior, the parental attitudes toward feeding, bowel training, and childhood sexuality, sibling rivalries, the internalization of parental attributes in ego and superego formation, etc.; and Freud's discovery of the oedipal configuration opened the way for study of the family dynamics. However, attention focused predominantly on the parent-child interaction, and even theories of the triadic oedipal situation rarely considered the interrelationships between parents. In practice, psychoanalytic treatment ranges beyond its theory and is concerned with the examination of how the parents' relationships with each other and with siblings has affected the patient. Knowingly or unknowingly, it deals with matters such as the cohesiveness and unity of the family, its way of communicating, its patterns of emotional reactivity, its taboos that influence what must be repressed, its standards, its relationships with the community, etc. Study of the family process forces explicit recognition of such factors and the extension of theory to include them. The family is a unit, and the actions of any member affect all; it has characteristics superordinate to those of its individual members; it subserves societal functions; it constitutes a milieu as well as a group of persons. The study of the development of the individual requires proper recognition of the family's functions as a social system to

[7]

rear children to live in social systems through internalizing institutions and learning social roles—those of others as well as their own. Viewing the personality development of a person in his family setting leads to interest in the relationship between the structuring of the ego and the structure of the social unit in which he grows up. Studies starting with the individual thus meet with sociologic studies of the family as a basic unit of society—and close the gap between biologically and societally oriented studies and theories of human behavior—a unification essential for a comprehensive understanding of human organization, motivation and behavior.

The first lecture, "The Family and Human Adaptation in the Scientific Era," examines the thesis that the isolated nuclear family, despite its paucity of stabilizing forces, is better suited for preparing its children to live in a society that is rapidly changing its adaptive techniques than are families with extended kinship systems. The argument might be extended to contend that a broad segment of the population can achieve a scientific orientation only after urbanization and industrialization have fragmented the extended family and diminished the hold of set patterns of child rearing and traditional techniques of adaptation by promoting marriages between persons of different cultural or subcultural origins. The instability of the isolated nuclear family can, however, reach such proportions that it provides insufficient structuring, security, and satisfaction for its members. The instability affects not only the stability of individuals raised in these families but also the stability of the society through undermining the family unit and the culture's ethical directives. As the trend toward isolated families cannot be undone, the continuity of this culture may well depend upon strengthening this unstable family form by gaining coherent concepts of what essentials of family life must be maintained.

The second and third lectures offer an approach to the question of what the family must provide to assure adequate adaptive capacities and ego integration in its offspring. In "Family Organization and Personality Structure," I propose that the essential dynamic structure of the family rests upon the parents' ability to form a coalition, maintain boundaries between the generations, and adhere to their appropriate sex-linked roles. Then I examine how failure to meet these few requisites leads to distortions in the ego structuring of their children. "The Family, Language, and Ego Functions" examines the requisite capacity of parents and the family they create to transmit the basic adaptive techniques of the culture. In this lecture, which has been reconceptualized and completely rewritten since its original informal presentation to a seminar at Tulane, I focus specifically upon the transmission of linguistic meanings, for they are essential for the communication and utilization of other instrumental techniques and critical to ego functioning in general—to the capacity to direct the self into the future. I examine theoretical and clinical evidence that limitations of the "mind" are often not deficiencies of the brain but of the linguistic and experiential symbols required for thinking, and that distortions of mentation can derive from the family environment.

After completing the third lecture, which utilizes the Whorf-Sapir hypothesis for much of its theoretical foundations, I suffered from misgivings because of the difficulties that are being encountered in validating Whorf's observations. However, some lengthy discussions with the Japanese psychiatrist, Dr. Takeo Doi, dispelled my doubts concerning the essential validity of the approach. Dr. Doi (1962) had sought to explain a few of the ways in which Japanese and American interpersonal relationships differed. He found it necessary to use a few Japanese words that have no English equivalents. For several of us to obtain a reasonable grasp of the word *amaeru* which denotes a person's need for another to be dependent upon him, the satisfying of this need in another, and also the wish for such dependency, it was necessary to spend four or five hours exploring differences in Japanese and American maternal attitudes, family configurations, educational incentives, employer-employee relationships, leisure time activities, religious beliefs, etc. At the end, the Americans recognized the absence of a fundamental concept in our culture as well as of a word in our language, but we were still uncertain whether we grasped the Japanese concepts accurately or were translating them into cultural as well as linguistic approximations.

The Family and Human Adaptation
in the Scientific Era

Today there are a number of areas of common interest to the sociologist and the psychiatrist—the hospital milieu and the influence of its social and political structure upon its members, both patients and staff; the relationship between social class and the occurrence and treatment of mental illness; the variation in personality with ethnic difference and culturally divergent child-rearing practices—to name but a few examples. I believe, however, that it is in the study of the family that the fields converge rather than simply share interests and benefits from collaborative work. It is the family that mediates between the individual and society, and the family that unites the biological and the cultural directives that enter into shaping the person. On the one side, psychiatry requires increased knowledge of the family as the matrix in which personality development and its deviations unfold; and on the other side, the social scientist must consider how the family reflects its societal matrix and serves to assure its stability and continuity.

My interest in the family arose from the clinical finding that schizophrenic patients had always been

[11]

raised in seriously disturbed family settings, and that other severely unstable patients also came from homes in which noteworthy imbalances between family members existed (Lidz, 1958). It seemed important to study the relationship between the family pathology and the individual psychopathology of its members, particularly of the children who had started their lives within these families. We found it necessary to leave our usual preoccupation with the individual and the vicissitudes of his personality development to seek to understand something of the fundamentals of family life. In so doing, we have maintained a clinical and tangible focus upon empiric material by studying intensively the natal families of schizophrenic patients (Lidz and Fleck, 1960). The serious disturbances of family structure and interaction observed in each of these families has led us to puzzle over what essentials are lacking that give rise to disturbances in virtually all areas of family functioning. The proper topic for me would concern the families of these patients, but I wish to go afield and consider, rather, some aspects of the dilemma of society in the scientific age, specifically those created by the changing nature of family structure. It is from contemplating the role of the family in the disorganization of our patients' personalities that I arrived at some thoughts concerning the role of the family in the dissolution of cultures.

Civilizations have died from many causes or through a concatenation of reasons—from the sheer ruthlessness of a handful of men, as in the case of the Incas, to a complexity of factors that led to the prolonged decline of Rome—factors that included overexpansion, invasion, malaria, soil erosion and the inability of men to cope with the multiple problems which, become intangible, could no longer be met through decision and conscious skill. Many students, however, have noted the correlation between the disorganization of a society "to hastening ills a prey," weakened through inner corruption, unable to absorb those it conquers, willing to relinquish its borders to the conqueror, and the dissolution of the family. Carle Zimmerman (1947) places the blame for the collapse of the family upon the decline in the moral character of peoples after a civilization has reached its zenith, particularly upon the degeneration of sexual morals when hedonism guides and the individual becomes unwilling to forego easy pleasure to assume the responsibilities of an enduring marriage and the burdens of parenthood. I believe, rather, that when a society expands to impinge upon and then incorporate other societies with different cultural ways, new influences can enter more rapidly than they can be absorbed. Then, a babel of cultural traditions develops; the value of the inherent traditional ways is doubted and then ridiculed; the sanctity of parental authority is lost; the society creates various institutions that take over many of the original functions of the family; and then the individual and his own welfare or pleasure gain precedence over collective needs of the family and of the society. I shall try to examine why the decline of the family is so dangerous to the continuity of a society.

Following the decline of Rome, the Christian fathers appear to have been keenly aware that the family formed the warp and woof of society and furnished the foundations for ethical behavior. They re-instituted the sanctity of marriage, placed a divine interdiction upon consorts, heterae, and homosexual liaisons, and required the procreation of children, banning the contraception, abortion, and infanticide that had been rife since the days of Augustus (Zimmerman, 1947). It is difficult to know how effective such measures were in re-establishing secure family life, for with the breakdown of a central government, a new need arose at a primitive, undirected level for the family as a basic structural unit to furnish security and provide for division of labor and economic exchange. The trustee family, building up to a feudal heirarchy, again preempted loyalty, and a new cycle was started. A trustee type of family could not, however, survive in an urban industrial setting. In Tuscany, where a type of industrialism was first established in Europe after the fall of Rome, the feudal family became a curse, leading to intra-urban warfare until the strongholds of these families were razed and the loyalty to the extended family was broken by the influx of new citizens into the industrial and commercial centers (Schevill, 1936).

On the other hand, civilizations can become decadent because customs cannot change, shielded from intruders or from the impact of invaders. In China, at least since the time of Confucius, the civilization rested on a filial family inculcating piety of children to parents and emphasizing education through learning the teachings of sages pertinent 2400 years before. It produced citizens with high ethical principles and a highly stable culture that resisted and engulfed those who came to conquer. The Great Wall existed within the family system as well as around the periphery of China. When the Chinese Communists today seek to obliterate the filial family, it is not simply for economic reasons or because they follow Engel's (1902) teachings that the family is a bourgeois device for enslaving women, but because they appreciate that a family that seeks to perpetuate tradition is inimicable to the rapid social and economic change they are seeking. The attempt in China to eliminate the family entirely, if indeed they really seek to do so, is almost bound to fail, even as it did in the early days of the Russian revolution (Timasheff, 1946).

The relationship of the family and its structure to the nature of the society in which it exists and to the ethos of the people forms an intriguing but a very large topic. I wish here only to focus upon some of the problems relevant to the atomistic family in the atomic age, or in terms I personally prefer, of the isolated nuclear family in the scientific age, and thereby enter upon some questions concerning the survival of our civilization and our culture.

To do so and in order to make clear my comprehension of the role of the family in the continuity of society and in the personality development of the individuals who comprise the society and carry its culture, I shall review a few fundamentals concerning the basis of man's adaptive capacities—his ways of coping with his environment and surviving its hazards, including those he so perversely insists upon creating for himself.

[15]

To understand man, his adaptation, and his dependence upon social systems, we must recognize that he possesses two endowments—a biological heredity established through the evolutionary selection of genetic mutations and transmitted through the genes from generation to generation, and a cultural heritage that is passed on interpersonally, that is, extragenetically to each new generation. The genetic evolution of man virtually ceased some twenty to thirty thousand years ago. For countless millennia before he assumed his present form, the process of evolution had favored the selecting-out of improvements in the brain and neuromuscular system that permitted the two interrelated attributes of tool-bearing and symbolic communication. These traits fostered survival better than other inborn equipment such as fur, agility in climbing, etc., that was sacrificed in the process. Eventually, the unique aspects of human adaptation depended upon the evolution of a brain that permits verbal communication and its internal counterpart—mentation.

Through his ability to manipulate symbols—words and visual images—instead of objects, man was freed from the consequences of acts in order to learn. As John Dewey (1929) stated, "he could act without acting" and go through trial-and-error procedures in his imagination rather than committing himself to the actual deed. He could gauge whether a club could suffice to subdue a foe and whether the encounter was worth risking. He could review his past experiences in his imagination, fragment and reshuffle them, utilizing the pertinent, and then project converging lines through the transitory present moment into the future. Even primitive man was something of a scientist in seeking to increase his security and gain control over the future, by predicting the chances on how events would turn out and how he could manipulate them.

According to Greek mythology, civilization started when Prometheus stole fire from the Olympians and bestowed it upon man—a first harnessing of nature to man's ends. Prometheus literally means "forward thinking" or foresight. When this attribute had been acquired, the history of the human race had started. We cannot here enter upon that inevitable consequence of the human condition, that with the foresight required for survival, man became burdened with concerns over the future, to live with anxiety over contingency and with awareness of his mortality.

The ability to select appropriate uses of his past, and choose from among the alternative paths into the future constantly being presented to him, released man from motivation based only upon impulsion by the immediate past and his present impulses, drives and wishes. He could strive toward projected ends and become more clearly impelled by future gains and objectives. He became goal-directed as well as drive-impelled, and acquired a new type of adaptation, a greater freedom of self-direction, and a capacity to develop value systems.

We cannot here trace the many consequences of man's capacity to think and thereby to gain increasing mastery over the remainder of nature, and decrease his vulnerability to its contingencies. Let us be clear

[17]

about one matter, however. To insist, as we must, that man is an animal, one of the countless species that have arisen and disappeared, is not to say man is *just* an animal. The emergence of the human species marked a decisive turn in the history of the world— and now of the solar system—for the switching system of his brain became a major switching system of nature. His purposes, his efforts to provide for his future, began to direct events. To use one simple example, the process of natural selection that controlled the evolution of new species of plants and animals was altered decisively by his planned cultivation of vegetables and breeding of animals. Gradually, the entire world has become his domain which he directs and rules to his ends.

Still, man's adaptation depends upon his ability to communicate as much as upon his thinking. Through speech, he can teach and direct others without being limited to the use of direct example. He could convey the fruits of his experience to the next generation and across generations, so that knowledge became cumulative. Animals learn, but what they gain is of little benefit to their descendants who must ever learn anew for themselves. Gradually, over countless generations, groups of people living proximately built up ways of coping with their environment and found ways of living together that formed their cultural heritage. This included the language itself, ways of thinking and reasoning, an image of their world, their customs— as well as the actual tools they created. Unless each biologically endowed infant grows into and assimilates the cultural heritage of his people, he becomes

[18]

no more capable of adapting to, and coping with, his environment or of living in society than were his pre-stone-age ancestors. Man as a biological organism has changed little in the past twenty thousand years, but the culture which he assimilates as he matures has changed profoundly—and therefore so has man as a person rather than as an animal.

If we turn matters around and consider society rather than the individual, each society has a vital interest in the indoctrination of the infants who form its new recruits. It lives only through its members, and its culture is its heart which they must keep pulsating. Without it, its members are rootless and lost, and they will defend it with their lives—but they must be so raised that the culture exists in them and they can transmit it to the next generation. It is a task that each society largely delegates, even though unwittingly, to an agent—the family.

Children do not grow up in the larger society of which they are members, but within a family that provides protection for them within the society. The biological make-up of the child—his prolonged helplessness and need for nurturant care that are necessary concomitants of his dependency upon his large brain and his capacity to learn for his major adaptive techniques—dictates that he be raised in a family by persons with a strong emotional attachment to him, to whom his needs are as important, if not more important, than their own, and who provide the essential care and protection until he can provide for himself adequately. While providing for the child's physical needs, the parental persons consciously, and even more unconsciously, convey to the child the mores of the society and its instrumental techniques for coping with its environment that it has built up over ages. They provide the fundamental training in emotional reactivity, in ways of relating and communicating with others, and for living in social groups. In the process, the personalities of these people who are essential to the child become part of the child through his identifications with them.

To the small child, the family ways and the parents' ways are *the* way of life and *the* way for people to interact with one another. Only after several years do other significant influences impinge upon him. The family influences are so pervasive and transpire so naturally that it has required the comparison of family patterns in divergent societies and, more recently, the study of the effects of serious family pathology to realize how greatly the individual is shaped by the family mold and how greatly the continuity of the society depends on the nature of its families. The family is, of course, far from the sole influence upon the child's development. All societies depend upon other institutions to enculturate the child beyond the family, and the need increases as a society becomes more complex. However, the family forms the first imprint upon the still unformed child and the most pervasive and consistent influence that establishes patterns that later forces can modify but never alter completely.

Most of what the child learns and acquires is not taught but conveyed implicitly as the child becomes ready, through physical maturation, to utilize his various inborn abilities; conveyed through the nature of the child's interaction with his parents; through example; through the child taking into himself the mother's ways as she cares for him, and the father's attributes as they affect him; and through the finding of a place for interrelating within the family into which he can grow without provoking conflict; by accepting the parents' dictates and restrictions to retain their love and care, by renouncing impulse and immediate gratification for the pleasure of a secure and happy relationship with them.

Now this indoctrination into ways of adaptation cannot be haphazard or left to chance. It must fit together to provide an integrated pattern of behavior suited to the biological needs and capacities of the child at different ages and at the same time suit the ways of the specific culture. The biological givens of the child set imperatives for the pattern. Unless the culture takes these into account it cannot survive. The needs of the parents set other requisites. The necessary nature of the family that divides it into two genders and two generations, both with differing functions within the family, also directs the structuring of families in all societies (Parsons and Bales, 1955). However, the family structure and its patterns for living together as a unit, and in harmony with the larger social system, is also a product of a long evolutionary process. In each society, a family pattern evolved suited to carry the society's traditions and its ways of living in its environment. The parents, having been raised in the society accept its customs as the proper way of life and tend to form families similar to those in which they had been raised.

I wish to consider, now, some aspects of the relationship that exists between the type of structure of the family in a given society and the adaptive techniques it conveys.

Let us first use a model, albeit a generalized and approximate model, of a nonindustrial society with a relatively nonmigratory population with an extended kinship system. It may be applicable to some very different family patterns within these limits such as the Mexican village family, the Hopi, the Fijians, the southern Italian peasant, etc. The nuclear family, i.e., the parents and their children, is not clearly demarcated from the larger network of relatives—grandparents, uncles and aunts, cousins, etc. The various functions of a family are shared by the relatives. The parents have help in raising their children, who, in turn, have many surrogate parents. The effects of eccentricities and deficiencies of parents, and, indeed, the influences of their individuality are minimized. Advice and support are readily available to the parents. At least one parent remains close to his or her natal family and the couple are not completely dependent upon each other for tangible and emotional support and complementation.

Parents who grow up in such extended families have ample opportunity to observe and practice child-rearing techniques. Further, as each parent is reared in a similar type of family and observes other families intimately, they enter marriage with relatively compatible expectations concerning the roles of husband

[22]

and wife and how children are to be raised. Few new influences enter to change the family pattern from generation to generation. The family here is an organization in which emphasis, both consciously and unconsciously, is placed upon the maintenance and transmission of a traditional way of adaptation that has evolved slowly. It is suited to a static society that does not foster such vices as curiosity, desire for improvement, or personal ambition. In Fijian villages that I have visited, concepts of individual advancement and of personal rather than collective gain are not even considered as a potentiality. This type of family provides security through furnishing clear patterns of how to live and how to relate to others. It inculcates an adaptive pattern suited to the environment and the circumstances in which the group lives and has lived, rather than providing adaptability to changing circumstances. Such patterns can perpetuate traditions that deter improved adaptation, and need not assure the happiness of the individual who may be enchained to a harsh lot in life, or be prone to develop an unhappy personality because of the child-rearing patterns. They may bring strife and violence into the lives of individuals, but the patterns of adaptation and the traditions of the society remain firm, changing but slowly.

This basic pattern of assuring adequate adaptation of each new generation can be disrupted by contact with other cultures, by conquest, by changes brought by population increase, etc., but its amazing stability and its resistance to change can be noted in many parts of the globe—outlasting and absorbing conquests by widely divergent civilizations, as in China or Sicily. The perpetuation of adaptive techniques, formalized and hallowed beyond question in the remote past and suited to different needs, leads to decadence when rigid custom suited to past eras rather than adaptive needs guides the people. In India, cows can roam the streets and hordes of baboons ravage the crops unmolested while children starve. The force of traditional ways upon a people engulfed by a society with a divergent ethos can contribute to anomie as has occurred in many American Indian tribes.

The current dilemma of the American family is very different. It derives, in part, from the rapid intermingling of ethnic groups in a new land in which none of the traditions was indigenous, and the breakup of broad kinship ties by immigration, migrations, and the demands of an industrial system that require its participants to follow opportunity. This rapid reshuffling of ethnic influences and fracturing of kinship ties contributed to making possible the unprecedented social mobility and scientific progress that has occurred. Concomitantly, major problems have arisen because of the rapidity of change in adaptive techniques that require a continuing reconstruction of what each new generation must acquire in order to fit into the changing society. The increased use of man's other basic mode of adaptation, his use of his intellect to master nature and to plan ahead, lessens the usefulness of the transmission of traditional ways. Tradition hampers readjustment, and a cultural lag can set in within a brief span of years—within a generation rather than over centuries.

How great has been the change brought by the scientific revolution? After all, for tens of thousands of years discovery and invention occurred infrequently and changes in ways of living came slowly. Indeed, the number of basic inventions prior to the eighteenth century are easily numbered—a handful, so to speak, per rise and fall of each civilization. Man could be prepared for life by learning what he had inherited in his tradition. Learning the wisdom given through revelation formed the foundation of one type of education which frowned upon innovation; and a classic education, a product of the Renaissance, primarily sought to regain the wisdom of the past. Trouble started, at least in Western civilization, when man sought to find and measure truth in terms of his own experience. Eventually, and it took a surprisingly long time, he consciously used his mind, his ability to think, as a means of improving his way of life, and began to systematize ways of thinking in order to discover and invent. The truth man pursued became less of a philosophical abstraction or a theological tenet than a truth measured according to whether it could help effect a change in his world or increase the predictability of events. While the Greeks made an effective start with scientific methodology, their concepts were limited and their experience was brief. The foundations for this major shift in adaptation were clearly stated by Francis Bacon (1955) during the late Renaissance in Elizabethan England, when he envisioned a totally new future for the human race if it would cultivate a scientific approach. The start was slow, but the new orientation began to pay off in the nineteenth century and has accelerated through to the present. We can currently appreciate the importance of the conscious use of the mind as a tool; it has become so vital to us that we create machines to augment the brain's capacities to record, sort out, and calculate—in itself a new phase of invention—without which we might be deprived of trips into outer space and the benefits of ballistic missiles.

Scientific thinking demands a willingness to follow observation and reasoning wherever they may lead, unfettered by traditional beliefs. Truth could no longer remain a "given truth" and the pursuit of truth in the scientific sense—that of seeking facts that increase the predictability and control of events—became a cornerstone of our techniques of adaptation and a foundation of our ethics. Known falsification in science, or even the denial of the ascertainable, has become immoral because we depend upon truth as best we can find it to gain security by planning ahead. The traditional concepts of man and his universe by which human beings had directed their lives for millennia slowly gave way and finally crumbled. Neither the way of life taught us as children, nor our ways of thinking about life, quite fit the world in which we live. And what do we convey to our children? Without tradition we are bereft of guidelines and flounder. With too great obedience to tradition, we cannot keep pace with the change.

Let us examine, now, how the scientific revolution has affected the family and its ability to convey the traditions essential for adaptation and to provide a stable foundation for the developing personality.

With the disruption of the extended family through migration, urbanization, and industrialization, the parents and their children are relatively isolated from their kin, and numerous tasks that were formerly shared by relatives fall to the parents alone (Bott, 1957). These parents, themselves raised in isolated family units, lack experience in rearing children, particularly when the mother has been educated primarily to pursue an occupation. Further, marriages in urban United States frequently cross ethnic, religious, and social class lines, and the parents who grew up in families with divergent customs, role allocations, and belief systems must fuse them into a new entity (Spiegel, Kluckhohn et al., 1954). The organization of the new family has not evolved over generations to assure the continuity of the cultural pattern into the raising of children suited to the life in the society. Whether or not it forms a satisfactory training ground at all depends largely upon the personalities of the two parents and how they fit together. It lacks the security provided by time-tried customs and the unconscious assurance that the way in which the family lives is the proper way.

The scientific tradition has influenced even those who are not scientists. Parents consider that the ways of the past generations are old-fashioned, outmoded, and did not provide them with a suitable preparation for life. The expert with his scientific approach to child rearing provides the authoritative pattern. The new methods are grafted onto old roots, sometimes producing strange blossoms. The fundamental principles advocated by experts have been changed radi-

[27]

cally at least three times during the past thirty years, preventing the establishment of a pattern from one generation to the next. Many conscious decisions leading to self-conscious practices have had to replace built-in and never-questioned patterns of child-parent interaction. Many of our insecurities in living and the instabilities of individuals surely arise from the contemporary family's difficulties in finding a secure structure and satisfactory ways of raising children.

However, despite its deficiencies, this isolated nuclear family reflects our current societal structure and is more suited to it than the extended family system. Indeed, in countries such as Japan that are seeking to catch up with the scientific era, the young generation consciously seeks to break the ties with the old family system. In our isolated families, each generation of parents and each set of parents alter the child-rearing procedures and the set of traditions they transmit, lessening the hold of rigid convention upon the new generation. The function of exogamy of assuring some degree of intermingling of family traditions as well as the constant admixture of genic lines has been heightened to the danger point. However, children raised in these more malleable families are likely to be more capable of adaptation to new and constantly changing conditions. In a sense, they are raised to live with change—to find new useful ways of adaptation rather than to seek answers from the past. It is a precarious way for a precarious world.

We may say that contemporary life requires adaptability rather than patterns of adaptation. Adaptability requires an ability to utilize intellect, to plan toward

[28]

the changing future rather than a need to adhere to ways inculcated in childhood or the patterns of parents' lives. But it also requires an emotional equilibrium that permits a person to be malleable, to adjust himself to others without fear of loss of identity with change. It requires a basic trust in others, and a confidence in the integrity of the self. The potentiality for adaptability cannot achieve realization if persons, individually or collectively, must be engaged in fighting old battles of childhood, seeking finally to gain what had been denied them then, rather than meeting new situations; seeking to hurt others because of the hurts of childhood, or, throughout adult life, seeking to reshape or repossess the past—the most futile of all human endeavors—rather than to shape the future.

The individual today has fewer persons upon whom he can remain dependent; fewer traditions that he can trust; less opportunity to follow in his parents' path; the need to leave settings in which he had built up secure relationships; fewer guides for relating to his spouse and for parental behavior. He is criticized for being outer-directed, for seeking conformity, for relying upon experts or advertising, for seeking psychiatric guidance; for voting for social security rather than being self-reliant. We are, indeed, when we consider his situation, placing great demands upon him—that is, upon ourselves.

It is at these times when the people turn from tradition as a guide for living, when the worth of ethical principles is constantly challenged, when the value of parental authority is doubted, and when many deci-

sions rest upon individual choice, that cultures of
the past have started to crumble. With basic emotional needs left unsatisfied within the natal family,
the adult requires more from the marital relationship than can be given by a spouse. The family offers
less to the child, and the child grown to adult is willing to sacrifice less for his family. Perhaps it is when
the security and contentment that derive from close
interpersonal relationships begin to fail, that a people turn to narcissistic gratification and hedonistic
choices. Marriage declines, divorce increases, the responsibilities of parenthood are avoided. The family
network that forms the matrix of society becomes
faulty and the family as a carrier of essential tradition declines.

Paradoxically, it is at just such times that the nuclear family gains in importance. The spouses become
more interdependent upon one another and the children's development rests more fully upon the parental guidance. The high divorce rate does not indicate that the importance and influence of the family
is declining, but rather that it now fills so many functions for the spouses, formerly shared by other institutions, that the strains upon the family are inordinate. If it cannot survive these strains, our society and
our culture are in graver danger than from any external foe. The American family, lacking a secure and
unified tradition and dependent upon the compati-
bilities of the personalities of the parents, has been
subject to many strains and insecurities that it transmits to the children it raises. Still, this form of family
life, despite its deficiencies, is surprisingly well suited

to the society in which it exists, that rests upon scientific progress. A return to a more static pattern would not suit contemporary needs. We require a family with the potential for change and yet with a basic stability, a family with a dynamic equilibrium.

Aware of the malleability of the child, we have sought to promote adaptability and stable personality integration by study of the child's needs and how parents can meet them. The scientific scrutiny of the child and the parent-child transactions has, despite errors inevitable in a new science, provided much sound and useful guidance to recent generations of parents. There has been, however, relative neglect of the family as a unit with an organization and needs of its own and in which the actions of any member affect all. The developing child is influenced by his family environment as a totality and not simply through the care he receives from individuals or by his dyadic relationships with other family members. The family as the basic social institution establishes the foundations and patterns of ways of relating to other social systems and a sense of the worth of human institutions. The value of marriage and parenthood, the worth or worthlessness of the roles of husband and wife, of mother and father, and even of maleness and femaleness are conveyed by the parents' relationships and the satisfaction and appreciation they derive from their roles. Ego ideals that the child strives to obtain as well as superego directives are based upon the family life. We are only beginning to appreciate the importance of family structure and the nature of its transactions both for the child and the integrity

[31]

of society. It is possible, even probable, that continued scientific scrutiny of the central position of the family in human relationships will eventually provide guidance that will gradually disseminate and influence family life even as the study of the infant and child has increasingly guided child-rearing techniques.

Let us try one simple example. Mothers have been blamed individually for much of what has gone wrong with their children, and collectively for many of the ills of society. "Momism" has been blamed for the high incidence of combat neuroses and lost battles (few generals are mothers), maternal rejection for schizophrenia, working mothers for juvenile delinquency, lack of maternal affection for alcoholism, drug addiction and peptic ulcer.

It is true enough that a secure and affectionate mother-child relationship provides the foundation for stable personality development, but let us look more closely to see if only the mother is involved. The changes in society and family structure which we have been considering surely have burdened the mother far more than the father. It is she who lacks the support of relatives in raising children and who feels the loss of early experiences in child rearing and homemaking. Further, we have just passed through an era of emancipation of women, but somehow the "feminist" movement seemed to mean making women more masculine. Equality of the sexes was too often taken to mean similarity of ability and opportunity. In gaining her rights, woman forsook many of the prerogatives and advantages of being a woman. She could have a career and help support the family, but this did not diminish the work or better qualify her for the tasks that she must carry out if she wishes to gain completion as a woman—as a wife and a mother. Anyhow, these are not functions a woman can carry out unaided; for in order properly to devote her energies in mothering and make the essential emotional investment of herself with her children, she has always required support, protection, and sources of emotional security. Today, there is typically no person other than her husband to supply these needs. Where is he? Often enough, doing his best to provide emotional as well as financial support, but more often preoccupied with his career or relaxing from it during evenings, and on the golf course where the family cannot follow on week ends, while his wife grows weary of the house and guilty of being tired of the children. The father, too, is important in the child's development, forming a model for a son to emulate if the mother cherishes him, and making a daughter feel that she can be loved as a woman, and through the affection and respect he gives his wife making womanhood desirable to the daughter (Lidz, Cornelison et al., 1957). The wife, to be an adequate mother, requires not only skills but to find pleasure in her work that comes from feeling supported, appreciated, and secure in her marriage. The deficiencies of the contemporary mother are not simply her personality shortcomings but part of the current dilemma of the family. A marriage is a union of a man and woman, two people who differ in many ways aside from their anatomy, who have different

[33]

ways of regarding the world, of what is desirable in life, and for relating to people, instilled in them from birth. They have different roles in life and are therefore incomplete alone, requiring completion from the other. It becomes increasingly evident scientifically, as it has been through common sense, that children require two parents with whom they interact and who optimally are of opposite sexes in temperament and outlook, but who together form a parental coalition complementing and completing one another.

If, as I have suggested, the decline of a civilization can follow upon the deterioration of its family life and the ensuing blurring of cultural traditions, it becomes apparent that man's way of adaptation is intimately related to his ethics. When the pursuit of individual gain and immediate pleasure takes precedence over regard for social institutions in a large proportion of the populace, the society totters. Individuals who cannot, when necessary, subjugate impulse and immediate gratification to more enduring objectives with consideration of the needs and regulations of the social system are classified as sociopaths deficient in superego controls. The superego, with its moral and ethical injunctions derived from internalization of parental guidance and authority, enables long-range adaptation through guiding beyond the moment to more enduring objectives and to gaining pleasure from the esteem and affection of others. Adequate superego development requires respect for parents and childhood security derived from family unity. Moral principles are largely concerned with

[34]

man's relationships to his fellow men even when presented in terms of his relationship to his God. An overemphasis upon other-worldliness and rewards of an afterlife contains elements of despair concerning the worth of interpersonal relationships on earth. If we seek a scientific basis for ethics, I believe we must begin with an examination of family life for it is here, in the relationships between parents and between parents and children, that the patterning of a person's relationships with others and with groups is laid down.

Within the family, moral principles have a definite and concrete meaning rather than forming abstract ideals. In this mutually interdependent group of persons, the behavior of any member affects all. Self-interest does not differ appreciably from the need to please and satisfy others—others whom one loves, or seeks to love even when one hates, and whose affection and support make life meaningful, and the absence of which breeds loneliness and despair. The hopes for their children's future happiness raise the parents beyond the present of their own lives into an interest in the future. Suffering visited upon the children is punishment for the parents. Yet, in general, the children grow to be trusting if their parents have been trustworthy; give affection and love if they have received it; rebel and seek to hurt if they are disillusioned; became devious if they can only gain their needs through circumvention. The child emulates unconsciously what the parents are, rather than what they pretend to be. The ethical behavior learned within the family does not depend as much upon precept as upon the character of the parents and the nature of the home they establish—upon who the parents are and how much of themselves they can give to those who need them and depend upon them.

It is not simply the ethics of individuals that are involved, but the continuity of a people as a nation or a culture. We have reason to be concerned that where an authoritarian family structure predominates, democracy rests upon shallow footings. The continuity of our own democratic way of life may well depend less upon what we teach in school and repeat in speeches than upon maintaining and fostering a predominance of families with parents who have respect and affection for their children and induce respect for authority but not submission to it; families in which parental omniscience does not squelch curiosity and the child's belief in his own ability to solve and master difficulties; in which the prerogatives of others are respected and there can be a striving for a common good. A "democratic family" does not mean voting on decisions, or a permissiveness of unchanneled freedom, but one of co-operative responsibility with appreciation and respect for the rights and needs, and, even the idiosyncrasies of others.

Summary

Man's adaptability and the continuity of the culture that carries his heritage of instrumental techniques both depend greatly upon the integrity of the family. The isolated nuclear family structure that has developed through industrialization and urbanization

[36]

is better suited than the extended kinship family for training its offspring for the adaptability required in a rapidly changing world, but deprived of the support of kin and secure tradition, it is an unstable unit. Its stability and capabilities depend primarily upon the personalities of the spouses who unite to form the family. However, the old extended family structure cannot be reinstituted, nor would it be suited to contemporary needs. Although, with sufficient time, a new and more stable pattern may evolve, the scientific era permits little respite from change. In a scientific era, the family requires intensive study by behavioral scientists to ascertain what is essential to the family everywhere and what is essential to foster our democratic heritage so that in a changing society, that will require future changes in the family, the requisites can be maintained. The task of understanding the fundamentals of the dynamics of family life will require time, and it will take even longer to influence family life significantly. It is an urgent matter. However, despite the ominous predictions of imminent dissolution of the family made during recent decades, there are indications that the family in the United States, even though perplexed and floundering, is regaining strength and vitality.

A larger proportion of the population is married than ever before. It appears as if people living in an insecure world in which values and purposes are obscure have intuitively realized that meaningful values can be found in the relationships between spouses and between parents and children. In contrast to expectation and prediction, couples are voluntarily seeking to have more children who provide clear and tangible tasks and purpose for existence. They are willing to commit themselves and their progeny to the precarious future. It appears that women, having won their emancipation, recognize that woman's self-realization is linked to marriage and child rearing. Despite the inevitable frustrations, and even despite tangible failures, the vast majority of persons seek a more enduring happiness in firm family relationships.

A clearer understanding gained through scientific scrutiny of the functions of the family and what is requisite to fulfill the needs of spouses and promote the harmonious development of offspring can help preserve the essentials while the family continues to change in a changing society.

Family Organization
and Personality Structure

THE INDUSTRIALIZATION of our society increasingly requires the nuclear family of parents and their children to exist in relative isolation from their extended families. Deprived of the support and guidance of kin, the structure and stability of the family depend greatly upon the personalities of the husband and wife and how they interrelate with each other. The spouses who have been reared in isolated families are uncertain of their roles as marital partners and parents and of the traditional patterns of child rearing. When they have grown up in families with different social and ethnic traditions, they have divergent concepts of marital and parental roles. Despite the insecurities of this family system, it contains the potential advantage, as I noted in the preceding lecture, of being suited for raising children trained for adaptability to rapidly changing circumstances rather than to rely primarily upon traditional patterns of adaptation. The stability of the family, which is essential to rearing secure and adaptable offspring, might be enhanced if the essentials of the family as a social system were more clearly understood. I shall seek to designate some characteristics of the family that appear critical for assuring the reasonable ego integrity and adaptability of children it produces and raises.

As reliance upon traditional techniques of child rearing has diminished with the changing nature of the family, developmental psychology and the psychoanalytic study of the child have offered new guidance to parents. Through study of the changing needs and capacities of the child as he matures, the critical tasks of each phase of development, the vicissitudes of childhood eroticism, the effects of various types and intensities of maternal nurturance, etc., scientifically based direction has been provided to parents. Scientific scrutiny has helped to dispel a number of traditional misapprehensions concerning feeding, bowel training, and manifestations of childhood sexuality. The importance of the mother's stability and security as a person and in relating to the child has received increasing emphasis. The child's internalization of parental attributes in his ego and superego formation has focused attention on the parental personalities and behavior. I shall not seek to review the many gains in the understanding of child development and the parental influences upon it. The importance of the family unit to the child's development has, however, received relatively little attention despite the central position the oedipal situation holds in dynamic psychiatry—the family as a social institution and a subsystem of the larger society in which it exists, and into which the child must emerge. The child does not develop into an integrated person capable of mature and independent existence simply by passing through each phase of development with

minimal trauma and fixation, but must gain a co-
hesive structuring of his personality by growing up in
a social organization—the family—that directs his integration by providing the proper channels into which
he can develop and by motivating him to grow into
them. I shall seek to clarify and illustrate this concept.

In our intensive studies of the intrafamilial environment in which schizophrenic patients grew up,
my colleagues and I found it necessary to direct our
attention to the influence of the family as a unit upon
the children developing within it as well as upon the
child-rearing techniques, the individual personalities,
and the dyadic relationships between members (Lidz
and Fleck, 1960). As had been anticipated, we found
that the mother-child relationship had often been extremely deleterious with some mothers unable to establish ego boundaries between themselves and their
children, some unable to provide proper nurturance
during the child's infancy, and many displaying a disturbing combination of imperviousness to the child's
feelings and communications while being inordinately intrusive into the child's life, impeding or de-
stroying his integrity and initiative. Often the child-
rearing practices were not just faulty but bizarre. It
required but little study of the fathers to realize that
they were just as often as seriously disturbed as the
mothers (Lidz, Cornelison et al., 1957a). Despite
Freud's (1913, 1923) early emphasis upon the father's
role in superego formation and character structure,
the paternal influences upon offspring had been seriously neglected in studies of schizophrenia. Disturbances had occurred in virtually all stages of the child's

[41]

development. Such panphasic disturbances were not due simply to fixations or frustrations at the earliest preoedipal stages that prevented proper passage through subsequent developmental phases, but also to continuing serious impairments of the parent-child interaction. The more we listened to family members and observed their interaction with one another, the clearer it became that difficulties existed in all areas of the family transactions. The family troubles were pervasive and enduring, influencing the functioning of all family members, both parents and children, throughout the patient's formative years. The failure of integration that we term schizophrenia could be related, it seemed, to the faulty integration of the family.

In this lecture, I shall not discuss the etiology of schizophrenia, but the contribution of studies of such families to the understanding of family functioning. In following our data, we were led to ask if there might not be something fundamentally wrong with these families whose children became so disturbed and if they might not lack some characteristics essential for proper child rearing. As we worked with the parents intensively, we gained a view of the patient's predicament from a different perspective than that usually afforded the psychiatrist, and came to appreciate that the insecurities and the unhappiness of the parents as individuals and as marital partners affected the way in which they related to their children through every phase of development. It appears obvious enough that a child's personality development is influenced profoundly by the marital relationship of his parents—perhaps so obvious that it has either been taken for granted or forgotten, and has never received careful scrutiny.

The way in which parents relate to one another not only affects the transactions between each parent and the child, but also establishes the pattern of the family as an institution. It is here that the child obtains his foundations in group living, in the meanings of social roles, and in learning the worth of social institutions. He is unwittingly involved in a multiplicity of social phenomena that leave a permanent imprint upon him. I shall only note a few to indicate their variety and scope. He gains a sense of the security that derives from belonging to a mutually protective unit, and finds reward in renouncing some of his own wishes for the welfare of the collectivity. He learns about hierarchical systems of authority, and about the relationship between authority and responsibility. He assimilates behavior patterns and feelings of worth that relate to the family's position in society. He learns the society's ways of communicating and a varying degree of trust in verbal and nonverbal communications. He not only experiences the changing roles and role statuses of a child and the expectations held for him at each phase of development, but also the roles of father and mother, husband and wife, man and woman, boy and girl, and how they interrelate and conflict. The family value systems, role definitions, patterns of interrelating, meaning systems, etc., enter into the developing child through the family's behavior more than through what its members teach or even consciously appreciate. The child's ego

[43]

becomes structured through such acquisitions and by the way the family's organization directs him into certain patterns and closes off other potentials, channelling drives and interests, permitting certain dependencies and requiring other independent capacities according to his age, sex, and position in the family.

In pursuing what is essential in the family organization for promoting stable ego organization in its offspring, I wish to examine briefly the cardinal functions of the family. To fill its divergent functions without disruptive conflict, the family in every culture has developed organization and structure. The reverberations of the evolution of a family institution that subserves the needs of the society, the parents, and the children are echoed in the Greek myths that hold before civilized man the tragedies that unrolled from generation to generation when primal passions disrupted the unity of the family, as in the terrible saga of the accursed children of Tantalus that started with the sacrifice of a son as food for the gods, and led through incestuous rape and vengeful and sacrificial slayings of children to the murder of Agamemnon and the matricide of Orestes. As Aeschylus recognized, man could only live in freedom after the sanctity of family relationships had been established.

Some authorities, even some governments (Engel, 1902; Timasheff, 1946), have concluded that the family has outlived its usefulness and its functions can be subsumed by other institutions. More often, the family is accepted as essential because of its child-rearing functions. I am, however, reasonably certain that we cannot understand the family and why it exists everywhere unless we recognize that it subserves three sets of functions which, though distinct, are also intimately interrelated. It is likely that no other institution can simultaneously fill these three functions. They cannot be met separately without radical changes in our social structure and without grave consequences. It is possible that these functions which are fundamental to human adaptation cannot be filled separately at all and must be fused in the family.

The family provides shelter and nurturant care for children and concomitantly directs their personality development. In so doing, it also fills a vital need for the society through enculturating the new members. The family subserves other societal functions as well that I shall not enter upon in detail. It forms a grouping of individuals that the society treats as an entity; it creates a network of kinship systems that help stabilize even an industrial society; it provides status, incentives, and roles for its members within the larger social system, etc. The nuclear family, however, is formed by a marriage and serves to complete and stabilize the lives of the husband and wife. These three sets of functions of the family—for the children, for the spouses, and for the society—though interrelated and in many ways complementary, can also conflict, and some degree of conflict between them is inevitable. I shall only note in passing the existence of opposing interests between the societal functions and those of spouses and children as occur when a husband is removed from the family to serve in the military forces, or when the prevalent belief systems of the broader social system oppose those of the parents.

[45]

I wish to focus primarily upon the relationship between the fulfillment of the spouses' needs in marriage and the capacities of the family to carry out its child-rearing functions properly.

There are many reasons why people marry—sexual passion, economic and status reasons, to have children or to legitimatize a child, etc. Although we currently consider that properly marriage should be motivated by love, we also know that marriage for romantic love is more or less idiosyncratic to modern western society. Basically, however, marriage is an almost universal phenomenon because of man's biological make-up and how he is brought up to reach maturity. Each person grows up in a family throughout a long period of dependency, forming essential bonds to those who nurture him, gaining an integrated ego structure by assimilating from them and internalizing their ways and attributes. But within this family of origin, he must be frustrated and cannot achieve completion as an adult. Minimally, frustration exists because within the parental family a person cannot become a parent with its prerogatives, nor can sexual gratification be united with affectional relationships. In the parental family, he has enjoyed the security of being a member of a mutually protective unit in which his welfare has been of paramount importance to his parents. He leaves the family with unresolved emotional attachments and strong unconscious motivations to bring closure to these emotional imbalances. He moves toward a new union with a person who sufficiently fills the image of the desired complementary figure to be transformed into it—a transformation more readily

[46]

achieved when his perception is blurred by sexual impulsion. In the marriage, he hopes to attain again the security afforded by a union in which his needs and his welfare are as important to his wife as her own, because her well-being and security are irrevocably connected with his.

Marriage also occurs because the human species is divided into two genders. They are drawn together by sexual impulsion, but also because the two sexes complement one another in many other respects. From earliest childhood the male and female are subjected to gender-linked role training and thereby acquire—if not also because of genetic and hormonal differences —different ways of viewing the world, of relating to people, of giving and receiving affection, as well as differing skills. In a broad sense, neither a man nor a woman can be complete alone. It is not that opposites attract, but that the two genders are raised to divide the tasks of living, and to complement, modify, complete one another, and to find common purpose in raising their children.

Spiegel and Kluckhohn (1954) in their studies of the family have placed particular emphasis upon the parents' deficiencies in achieving reciprocal role relationships because of ethnic and social class disparities between them (Spiegel and Bell, 1959). While the approach has been useful and illuminating, in our studies we found that the couple's difficulties in gaining reciprocal relationships and mutual satisfaction arose more commonly from the unfilled needs they carried with them from their parental families that led to expectations that the spouses could not meet.

[47]

They also brought with them incorporated in their personalities other residues of their lives in their natal families—its traditions, role allocations, examples of marital and parent-child interaction, and the problems and conflicts in which they had been caught up (Lidz and Cornelison, 1958a). Some of the discrepancies between the spouses that could not be properly resolved derived from cultural differences, but often enough simply from the pathology of the relationships in their natal families that continued in their own personalities and personality needs.

Parsons, Bales, and their co-workers (1953, 1955) have abstracted, on the basis of theory, some of the essentials of family structure, and have indicated how failures to maintain this structure, based essentially upon the different roles and tasks of the two generations and two sexes in the family, lead to pathological family interaction. We have been seeking to examine how the disturbances in the personalities of the parents as individuals and as a marital couple lead to defects in the organization of the family they create.

In the families of schizophrenic patients which we studied, one or both spouses was seriously disturbed, and the influence of personality problems of marital partners upon the family organization was brought to attention sharply. Their needs, vulnerabilities, and pathological defenses may have precluded establishment of a satisfactory family life with any spouse, and usually their difficulties had led to the choice of a mate who also had serious problems. Psychiatrists frequently assume that no matter how inappropriate the choice of a mate seems, it fills some unconscious need.

[48]

The adage can be interpreted too broadly. The need may be to get away from the parental home immediately with pursuit of the first potential partner, or for the woman to find a man who will unknowingly become the father of the baby she is carrying. The unconscious need may be to repeat a neurotic pattern that will inevitably lead to frustration, and the motivating need may be satisfied but leave many other relational needs unfilled.

The majority of the marriages of the parents of our patients were highly schismatic, filled with chronic overt conflict and mutual devaluation of the spouse. The partners were unable to achieve a mutuality of purpose in major areas of living or workable reciprocal role relationships. Some failed to form a true nuclear family because both spouses retained primary loyalties to their families of origin, fighting any pull away from it and resenting the partner's intrusions into such dependence upon the parental home. However, not all of the families suffered from such clearcut marital disharmonies. In marriages which we have termed "skewed," the partners are reasonably well satisfied but the marital and parental roles are unbalanced and deviant (Lidz, 1957b). A marriage can be satisfactory to the husband and wife with all sorts of role allocations and ways of achieving reciprocity. The customary roles of male and female can be reversed with the wife supporting and the man cooking and housekeeping; they can each remain in their parental homes; one or both may find sexual outlets only outside the marriage either heterosexually or homosexually; one spouse may fill a parental rather than a

[49]

marital role for the other; it can form a sadomas-
ochistic partnership or a source of masochistic satisfaction to both. The variants are countless, and every
psychiatrist continues to encounter new permuta-
tions. However, when the arrival of children turns
a marriage into a nuclear family, the spouses' ways
of relating must shift to make room for the children,
and definite limits are set upon the couple's ways of
relating if they are also to foster the proper development of their children.

The study of a marital relationship, as complex as
it is, can be encompassed in terms of the interaction
of two persons. The family, in contrast, cannot be
grasped in terms of a dyadic relationship for it forms
a true small group with a unity of its own. As in all
true groups, the action of any member affects all and
the members must find reciprocally interrelating roles
or conflict ensues (Spiegel, 1957). The group as a
unit exacts loyalty requiring that each member give
some precedence to the needs of the group over his
own desires; and it requires unity of objectives, and
leadership toward these objectives. Small groups, even
threesomes, tend to divide up into dyads (Mills, 1953;
Strodtbeck, 1954) that exclude others from significant
relationships and transactions and impair or disrupt
the group unity. Structure, rules, and leadership are
required to minimize these divisive tendencies. Such
requisites of groups in general are heightened and
tightened in the family by the intimate living, and the
intense and prolonged interdependence of its members. Parsons and Bales (1955) moved from the study
of small groups to the study of the family. They

posited that the family, as most groups, would include two leaders who complement one another, an instrumental leader and an expressive leader, which they found in the roles of the father and the mother. It seems likely, however, that groups commonly have both types of leaders because the original group for all its members was a family containing a father and a mother, even as other social role relationships are first patterned in the family.

The family is, moreover, a very special type of group with characteristics imposed upon it by the biological relationships of its constituents and the purposes it serves. Recognition of these characteristics leads to an appreciation of some of its requisite structure.

1. The nuclear family is composed of two generations, each with different needs, prerogatives, and tasks.

(a) The parents, having grown up in two different families, seek to merge themselves and their backgrounds into a new unit that satisfies the needs of both and completes their personalities in a relationship that is permanent for them. The new social unit differs to a greater or lesser degree from their families of origin, thus requiring malleability in both partners. Further, the new relationship demands the intrapsychic reorganization of each spouse to take cognizance of the partner. To state the matter simply in psychoanalytic structural terms, the id, ego, and superego of each is modified by those of the partner, and the ego functions of each involve the well-being of the partner and the maintenance of the union.

[51]

(b) The children receive their primary training in group living within the family, remaining dependent upon the parents for many years, forming intense emotional bonds to them, and developing through assimilation from the parents and introjection of their characteristics, and yet must so learn to live within the family to enable them to emerge from it and start families of their own as members of the parental generation.

(c) The parents serve as guides, educators, and models for offspring. They provide nurturance and give of themselves so that the children can develop. Though individuals, as parents they function as a coalition, dividing roles and tasks in which they support one another. The parents are properly dependent upon one another, and the children must be dependent upon parents, but parents should not be dependent upon immature children.

2. The family is also divided into two genders with differing but complementary functions and role allocations as well as anatomical differences. The feminine role derives from the woman's biological structure and is related to nurturance of children and the maintenance of a home, leading to emphasis upon interest in interpersonal relations and emotional harmony—an expressive-affectional role. The male role is related to the support and protection of the family and leads to an emphasis upon instrumental-adaptive leadership characteristics (Parsons and Bales, 1955).

3. The bonds between family members are held firm by erotic and affectional ties. The parents forming a permanent union are permitted and even ex-

pected to have sexual relationships. While all direct sexual relationships within the family are prohibited to the children, erotic gratification from parental figures that accompanies nurturant care is needed and fostered, but must be progressively frustrated as the need for such primary care diminishes lest the bonds to the family become too firm and prevent investment of interest and energy in the extrafamilial world (Parsons, 1954).

4. The family forms a shelter for its members within the society and from the remainder of society. Theoretically, at least, members have the emotional security of acceptance because of affectional ties rather than because of achievements and have less need for defensive operations within the family group than in the external world. However, the family must reflect and transmit the societal ways—including its child-rearing techniques appropriate to each developmental phase, its meaning and value systems, etc.—to assure that the children can function when they emerge from it into the broader society.

These fundamental characteristics of the nuclear family, and corollaries derived from them, set requisites for a marital relationship if it is to provide a suitable setting for the harmonious development of its offspring. What appears to be essential can be stated simply, and may sound all too simple until we explore the consequences. The spouses need to form a coalition as members of the parental generation maintaining their respective gender-linked roles, and be capable of transmitting instrumentally useful ways of adaptation suited to the society in which they live.

[53]

It is obvious that parents must also possess techniques for rearing the child, if not also the emotional capacities to relate appropriately to him at each phase of his development. However, I am here primarily concerned with how the marital interaction influences the family organization and interaction. In seeking to cope with the vast topic, I shall consider only the parental coalition, and the maintenance of generation boundaries and gender-linked roles by the parents.

It is my thesis that a large proportion of the failures of adequate ego integration arises in persons who have grown up in families which lacked proper integration because the parents' ways of interacting led to a faulty family organization deficient in these essentials.

The Parental Coalition

The stability of the isolated nuclear family and the security of its members depend upon the strength of the parental coalition. The parents each have differing roles and functions but they interrelate to form a unit in regard to the children. When the marriage is working properly, each parent supports the other's role, increasing the assurance and strength with which it can be carried out. The mother can properly invest her energies in the care of the young child when economic support, status, and protection of the family are provided by the father. She can also better limit her cathexis of the child to maternal feelings when her wifely needs are satisfied by her husband.

The structural organization of the family also depends upon the appropriate sharing of roles by the parents while forming a coalition. The tendency of groups to divide up into dyads that create rivalries and jealousies is diminished if the parents form a unity in relating to their children. Thus, the major focus of the child's divisive efforts remains firm. The child is also provided with adult models who treat one another as alter egos, striving for the partners' satisfaction as well as for their own. The parent's inclusion of the other parent into the relationship with the child sets a pattern of group interaction that enables the family to form a solidary unit.

The parental coalition helps structure the child's ego development by frustrating his oedipal fantasies of dividing the parents to possess one and get rid of the other, and by directing him to the reality which requires repression and redirection of such drives and wishes. The child grows up valuing marriage as a source of support and emotional gratification, and thus gains a long-range goal to pursue. Concomitantly, he learns how marital and parental roles interrelate rather than exclude one another.

The child properly requires two parents: a parent of the same sex with whom he identifies and who forms a role model to follow into adulthood, and a parent of the opposite sex who becomes a basic love object and whose affection provides the child with a sense of worth. However, the value of the two parents is greatly diminished if they do not form a coalition. The parent of the same sex is not likely to be an acceptable role model if devalued by the parent of the opposite sex, whose love the child seeks; nor can the latter become a suitable model of a love object if constantly castigating and depreciating the parent with whom the child identifies.

Parents can, of course, form a reasonably satisfactory coalition in respect to their children despite marital disharmony, to some extent even despite separation. They can maintain agreement about how the children should be raised. They can even support their spouses to the children as worthwhile persons and good parents, as when a mother tells a child that her husband is a good father and a fine man whom she has loved, but that their ways and ideas differ.

In the highly schismatic marriages of parents of schizophrenic patients which we studied, the marriages were not simply unhappy: the spouses were hostilely depreciative of one another, rivalrous for a child, considering loyalty to the other parent as rejection, and making it clear that growing up to be like the other parent would be unacceptable. The pseudo-coalition that existed in the "skewed" families in which one parent abdicated the parental role—usually the husband who was but an adjunct to a disturbed but dominant wife—created serious role imbalances and promoted unhealthy dyad formation between mother and son.

The serious failures of coalition of parents of schizophrenic offspring permit a clearer view of the effects upon children than a study of lesser disturbances. The growing child may invest his energy and attention in seeking to bridge the gap between the two parents, or may feel responsible for satisfying the needs of both. Commonly, the child focuses on supporting or completing the life of a parent he needs rather than investing his energies into his own ego development. Often, the child becomes a scapegoat. His difficulties are magnified into the major source of dissent between the parents, and he comes to feel responsible for it. At times, the child falls in with the assignment and obliges by creating further unhappiness that masks the friction between the parents. The child who seeks to satisfy both parents can be caught in a "bind" (Weakland, 1960) in which behavior that satisfies one parent elicits rebuff from the other. The ramifications are many and I shall seek to illustrate rather than enumerate further.

Mr. and Mrs. N. had become emotionally estranged shortly before the birth of their daughter, Dora, who later became schizophrenic. The marriage had suffered from its inception by the discrepant personalities of the couple, and their intense loyalties to their parents and siblings. Mr. N. was highly narcissistic, an outgoing man who required demonstrative affection to support his self-esteem. His wife was an aloof, penurious, rather misanthropic woman with a sharp tongue, and was subject to depressive mood swings. Despite disagreements, the N.'s had managed to remain reasonably compatible for several years. Mrs. N. was very pleased with her older child, a son, and was very attentive to him. Five years after the marriage and just a few months prior to Dora's birth, a feud arose between their respective families when Mr. N.'s father was accused of dealings that led to the business failure and suicide of Mrs. N.'s father. Both Mr. and Mrs. N. became deeply resentful that the other sided with their own parental families, or, more accurately, did not side with the spouse against their own families. Though they continued to live together, the marriage became a hostile encounter in which open

[57]

conflict was avoided by mutual withdrawal. In the ensuing seventeen years, weeks would pass when they would not speak to one another.

During her pregnancy with Dora, Mrs. N. suffered an injury to her back that she blamed on her husband's neglect. Supposedly because of this incapacitation, she could not take care of Dora during her first two years of life, leaving her care to a maid. Later, she sought to be a good mother but rapidly lost patience. As her marital unhappiness mounted, she became increasingly critical of the child's behavior. When Dora became very trying after the age of twelve, Mrs. N. expressed frank hatred of her, and suggested dual suicide. In contrast, Mr. N., feeling neglected by his wife, turned to his daughter for the affection he lacked, lavishing affection upon her with much physical demonstrativeness. He would hug and kiss her excessively and often lie upon her bed until she fell asleep. Dora would climb into her father's bed when she became frightened during the night, until she learned the facts of life during adolescence, and feared she would become pregnant.

Mr. N. was highly critical of his wife, letting his daughter know that he had little regard for her mother, and constantly deprecated her to the children. Mrs. N., in turn, was withdrawn from her husband, angered by his neglect, and expressed despair at being tied to the marriage. The family situation was aggravated because Mr. N. avoided the unpleasant atmosphere and quarrels by spending most evenings at his club, encouraging his wife to believe he had a mistress. Despite intense feelings that his wife's attitude toward their daughter was rejecting and destructive, he assumed little responsibility himself.

In this marriage, as in the other schismatic families of schizophrenic patients, the parents openly and covertly undercut and devalued one another rather than formed a parental coalition. Mrs. N. may have had difficulties in being maternal to a daughter because of her own dissatisfactions with being a woman. Even more clearly, she had little empathy for her child because she was caught up in her enmity for her husband and filled with despair over her marriage. The more pleasure her husband gained from the child, the more embittered Mrs. N. became toward the girl. Mr. N., in turn, knew that his attentions to Dora angered his wife. Dora became a weapon through which they could express their resentment toward one another. Mrs. N.'s self-esteem, never too secure, fell with her husband's criticism of her, and his use of Dora's instability as evidence of her inadequacies as a mother. The parents helped demolish each other's parental value to Dora. Dora's identification with her mother was impeded by her mother's aloofness and resentment. It was blocked further by her father's constant castigation and deprecation of his wife. To remain acceptable to the father and to gain his love, Dora would have to seek to differentiate herself from her mother—a negative directive—instead of seeking to emulate her as a positive model of a woman who could gain the love of a man like her father. The split between the parents permitted Dora, with her father's help, to cross the generation lines and seek to replace her mother, leaving her prey to incestuous fantasies and fears during adolescence. Consciously or unconsciously, she became the major source of overt conflict between her parents. This permitted them to disregard their more fundamental incompatibilities, but also helped preserve Dora's dyadic involvement with her father.

Other girls cannot seek or cherish the affection of a father who is neglecting and hostile to a mother who provides protection and affection. In either case, the girl gains a strange impression of the woman's role in marriage and finds it difficult to develop toward filling the roles of wife and mother. Similarly, the resolution of a boy's oedipal involvement will be distorted if he does not rescind his ties to the mother, and seek to grow into a person who can gain a suitable love object like his mother by taking on his father's attributes. If the mother conveys hatred or contempt for the father and teaches disregard for him, a son is unlikely to identify strongly with his father.

More often than is apparent from casual study, children reared in divisive families develop a split in their ego structure. Two parents who are irreconcilable in reality become irreconcilable introjects. To maintain integrated functioning, the child develops alternative ego and superego formations. Let us consider a young woman whose first few years of life had been reasonably harmonious and happy when she was the pride of two doting parents. Then, her father began absenting himself from the home and his business, passing his days with a series of mistresses. He made it clear during the ensuing fifteen years that his wife was a cold and undesirable sexual partner. The mother expressed her hostility over his periodic desertions, his repeated business failures, and his girl friends. She found solace in her daughter, sleeping with her to exclude her husband, and telling the girl that she only continued to live for her sake. The girl, as an adolescent, found security in her mother's intense need for her, feeling that her mother would never abandon her as the father did. Still, she was burdened by her mother's depressive and obsessive ways, and delighted with her father's carefree attitude that made the family's very real troubles seem insignificant.

She identified strongly with the mother, whom she needed, and remained intensely tied to her, seeking to be a worrisome, industrious woman who would share her mother's concerns, eschewing sexual desire which her mother found so disgraceful in her father. In so doing, however, she felt worthless as a woman and unlovable to men. She decided to become a schoolteacher who would never marry. In her fantasy life, and on one isolated occasion in actuality, she was a very different person. She became involved in a romantic love affair, giving herself with such intensity to a youth, whom she consciously recognized as closely resembling her father in appearance and temperament, that she frightened him away. She was then identifying with her father's mistress, seeking to be the woman her father could love—a woman very different from her mother. Soon, she felt that she was deserting her mother and killing her, even as the father's mistress had been "killing" her mother. She gave up seeking to identify with the mistress—only to continue to live this other life in her daydreams, while chronically unhappy with her everyday life. Such partial splitting of the personality is far from uncommon. I believe that such problems can be

[61]

traced to the alternative integrations suited to the discrepant needs or patterns of the two parents.

When the parents cannot complement and support one another, at least in their parental roles, family tensions, role conflicts, and splitting into dyads become almost inevitable, and unity of leadership which in the family requires fusion of both maternal and paternal functions is lacking. Concepts of the roles of man and woman, of husband and wife, of father and mother, as well as the meaning of marriage and of parenthood are inculcated in the child basically through the examples of parental interaction.

The Maintenance of Generation Boundaries

Failure to achieve a parental coalition will often lead to infractions of the generation boundaries within the family. The division into two generations provides a major structuring influence upon the family. The parents are the nurturant and educating generation who give of themselves so that the child can mature and develop, providing for the child adult models to emulate, characteristics to introject, and interactional patterns to follow. Parents can and should be dependent upon one another, but not upon the immature child. The child needs the security of dependency to utilize his energies for his own development. His development can be stunted if he must emotionally support the parent he needs for security.

The division into generations lessens the dangers of role conflict by providing different roles for parents and children. It furnishes space free from conflict with a parent into which the child can develop. Different types of affectional relationships exist between parents than between a parent and child. Yet the situation is complicated because of the intense dyadic relationship heightened by erogenous feelings that properly exists between the mother and each pre-oedipal child, and by the slow differentiation of the child from his original symbiotic union with the mother. The generation division serves to aid both mother and child in overcoming the bond—a development that is essential to enable the child to invest in learning and peer groups and in gaining his own identity.

Serious failures to maintain the essential generation boundaries occurred in every family of our schizophrenic patients. This generalization includes the childlike dependency of one parent upon the other, the rivalries between parents for the affection and loyalty of a child, the intense parental jealousy of a child, and incestuous proclivities of a parent with a child, including mothers who rid themselves of a husband's desires by offering a daughter as a substitute. Indeed, it was the prominence of this finding that originally led to the scrutiny of how disruptions of the essential family structure can lead to disorganization of a child's ego development.

When, for example, a parent uses a child to fill needs unsatisfied by the spouse, the child can seek to widen the gap between parents and insert himself into it. He finds an essential place in completing the life of a parent and need not—and perhaps cannot—turn to the extrafamilial world for self-completion. The oedipal situation remains unresolved, for its proper completion depends upon having a family in which the parents are primarily reliant upon one another or upon other adults, and can therefore give of themselves to the child. When, in a schismatic marriage, one parent feels excluded, the child's fears of retribution and retaliation are not simply projections of his own wishes to be rid of a parent, but are based upon the reality of having a jealous and hostile parent.

When one partner is more of a child than a spouse, as often occurs in skewed marriages that are distorted because one spouse accepts the strange and paralogical ways of the more dominant partner, and depends upon the other for guidance and nurturance, the passive partner offers an ineffectual role model for a child, particularly for a child of the same sex. A father who seeks mothering and offers his wife little except the satisfaction of her needs to mother, and who exerts little authority in the family, offers a weak figure for a son to emulate. Further, as he is more of a child who can be displaced than a father figure whose prerogatives with the mother must be recognized, a son's transition through the oedipal situation may be impaired. Other such fathers are apt to be rivalrous with sons—an unequal competition. One father, for example, could not tolerate it when his wife sought to provide for the essential needs of their infant son. He constantly demanded attention, leaving his wife torn between them in her efforts to placate both. Later, he belittled his son's efforts in athletics. He attempted to teach him by demonstrating his own prowess and deprecating his son as awkward and sissified. Such rivalry, particularly when accompanied by poorly masked hostility, requires the son to give up efforts to achieve masculine assets lest they arouse the father's hostility.

A mother who cannot establish clear ego boundaries between herself and the child, as has been noted in many mothers of schizophrenic sons, is also violating the generation boundaries (Lidz and Lidz, 1952). Her son is to live out the life closed to her as a woman, and her husband fills a subsidiary role. She cannot clearly differentiate between her own needs and anxieties and those of her son. Under such conditions, children have difficulty in becoming discrete individuals for they are living their mothers' lives rather than their own; and they learn that they are not to grow up to be like their fathers, for these fathers are simply the mothers' means of having children and providing for them.

The maintenance of a strong erotic bond between mother and daughter does not occur as commonly as between mother and son. However, incestuous and near incestuous father-daughter relationships are probably more common than either of such mother-child relationships. A daughter having rescinded and repressed her primary attachment to the mother can find a new love object within the family in the father. The frustration of this relationship at or before puberty depends either upon the girl's recognition of the mother's priority with the father, or upon the father's capacity to maintain the generation boundaries. The N. family provided an illustration of a situation in which neither requisite was filled.

[65]

When the generation boundaries within the family are confused, the ensuing role conflicts distort the child's ego development in many ways, some of which have been indicated. The child's proper place within the family is invaded. Rivalries with parents absorb energies and foster internalized conflicts. A parent's dependency upon a child occupies the child prematurely with completing the life of another rather than with developing his own ego structure defined by clear boundaries. Aggressive and libidinal impulses directed toward parents become heightened rather than undergoing repression and gradual resolution, and are controlled only through strongly invested defense mechanisms.

The Maintenance of Sex-Linked Roles

The achievement of a workable coalition between parents usually depends upon the ability of both to assume their respective gender-linked roles in general accord with the cultural pattern and to permit the other to fill his or her role. As I noted earlier, some couples can achieve a reasonable reciprocity filling deviant roles but their children's development will be affected deleteriously.

The division of the nuclear family into two generations and two sexes creates, as Parsons and Bales (1955) have emphasized, four different role allocations. It not only lessens role conflict, but provides directives for the child's development. However, the value of maintenance of proper gender roles by parents is diminished when the parental coalition fails and the male or female role, as reflected in the parental relationship, is depreciated, deleterious, or even dangerous. The four role allocations do not, of course, provide for rivalries between children of the same sex, but rivalry between those of opposite sexes is fostered when the child can find little value in seeking to identify with the parent of the same sex.

The maintenance of the appropriate sexual roles by parents in their coalition plays a major role in guiding the child's development as a male or female. Security of sexual identity is a cardinal factor in the achievement of a stable ego identity. Of all factors entering into the formation of personality characteristics, the sex of the child is the most decisive. Confusions and dissatisfactions concerning sexual identity can contribute to the etiology of many neuroses and character defects as well as perversions. Probably all schizophrenic patients are seriously confused in this area. The assumption of proper sex-linked role attributes does not occur simply because a child is born a boy or a girl, but is acquired by role allocations that start in infancy, role assumptions, and identifications as the child grows older (J. G. Hampson, 1955 and J. L. Hampson et al., 1955). Certain inherent difficulties potentially face both boys and girls in achieving firm sexual identity. The rebelliousness of the girl because of penis envy and the social limitations imposed by being a female have been emphasized in psychoanalytic theory. The boy, however, starts life in a symbiotic union with his mother, identifies with her, and experiences her as an omnipotent figure. Later, he experiences regressive tendencies to be cared for by

[67]

her, but must grow up capable of providing for a woman (Fleck, Lidz et al., 1963).

Clear-cut role reversals in parents can obviously distort the child's development, both when they are marked in the sexual sphere, as when the father or mother is an overt homosexual, or when they concern the task divisions in maintaining the family. A child whose father performs the mothering functions both tangibly and emotionally while the mother is preoccupied with her career can easily gain a distorted image of masculinity and femininity. The more common problem is more subtle. Talcott Parsons states that the female role is expressive-affectional and includes concern with the emotional homeostasis of her household, while the father is more concerned with instrumental tasks. A cold and unyielding mother is more deleterious than a cold and unyielding father, while a weak and ineffectual father is more damaging than a weak and ineffectual mother (Parsons and Bales, 1955). More explicitly, a cold and aloof mother may be more detrimental to a daughter who requires childhood experience with a nurturant mother to attain the maternal characteristics of a woman; and an ineffectual father may be more deleterious to a son who must overcome his initial dependency upon his mother to gain security in instrumentally providing for a wife and children. While the sharing of role tasks has become more necessary and acceptable in the contemporary family, there is still need for the parents to maintain and support one another in their primary sex roles.

The parents in the N. family, whose failure to form

[68]

a parental coalition and maintain generation boundaries has been discussed, provided poor guidelines for their daughter's achievement of secure sexual identity. Mrs. N., disillusioned in her marriage and depressed because of her resentment toward her husband, could not provide maternal care for her infant daughter. Having grown up in a large family in which the girls had felt unwanted and neglected in favor of the boys, Mrs. N. had little self-esteem as a woman and was unable to feel satisfaction in having a daughter. Her attacking, vindictive, and superior behavior toward her husband and her hostility toward her daughter provided a poor model of feminine and maternal behavior. Both her vulnerable self-esteem and her worth as a mother were further denigrated by Mr. N.'s castigations of her as a wife and mother, his almost studied efforts to enrage her, and his pretense of replacing her with a mistress.

A child's difficulties in identifying with a parent of the same sex because this parent is unacceptable to the other parent whose love the child seeks can be heightened by the homosexual tendencies of a parent. The mother may be basically unacceptable to the father who has homosexual trends simply because she is a woman. The daughter responds by seeking to be boyish, or to gain father's approval by being intellectual, or through some other means that do not threaten him by feminine appeal. Similarly, if the mother is consciously or unconsciously rivalrous with all men, a son can easily learn that masculinity will evoke rebuff from her, and the fear of engulfment or castration by the mother becomes a greater and more realistic source of anxiety than fears of retaliatory castration by the father.

While deficiencies in maintenance of appropriate sex-linked roles often concern the personality structure of the individual parent, or the mutual choice of spouses who complement each other, the difficulties can be aggravated by the refusal of a parent to permit the other to fill the appropriate position in the family. A man who married a woman who came from a trio of sisters, who were all contemptuous of men, may have had a suitably weak and masochistic character at the time of marriage, but he was denied sexual relationships by his teasing wife, ridiculed when he sought to make decisions for the family, and his career always was a secondary consideration to the wife's need to remain close to her dominating sisters who supported her in her contempt of her husband. The older son grew up to please women with his effeminate interests, despising his father. The younger son clung to the father who mothered him, and came to fear all women as he did his castrating mother and her sisters.

Although other factors can foster difficulties in achievement of secure gender role and identity—such as parents conveying the wish for the child to be of the other sex, and the avoidance of incestuous entanglements—a general assurance of a proper outcome is provided when the parents adequately fill their own gender roles and each is accepted and supported, if not cherished, in living out these roles within the family.

I have discussed problems of gender identity primarily in terms of roles and reciprocal role relationships, but I believe that the emphasis can readily be transferred to concern with the child's internalization of an ego ideal suited to the child's sex which serves to direct ego growth and stabilization.

Family Interaction and Resolution of the Oedipal Situation

Both Flugel (1921) and Parsons (1954), who studied the family from a psychoanalytic orientation, emphasized the precarious balance that exists between the affectional and erotic bonds that make for cohesion between the members of the nuclear family and are essential to the normal development of children, as against incestuous impulses that are disorganizing to the family and create both role conflicts between its members and intrapsychic conflicts within them. The oedipal situation occupies a central position in psychiatry because it is at this period that the child crosses a path with potential disaster on both sides. His development will be stunted or distorted unless he has received affectionate nurturant care—erotically motivated nurturance that has evoked sensuous pleasure in him—during his preoedipal phases. Then, as he completes his training in primary socialization and prepares to emerge into a life with his peers in play and at school, the erotic quality of his attachment must gradually be frustrated and the parent-child relationship freed of sexuality. This desexualization of the child-parent attachment is a cardinal task of the family. I do not believe that the repression of the erotic ties depends primarily upon a biological subsidence of the sexual drive at the time of resolution of

[71]

the oedipal situation, or upon the child's fears of castration or retaliatory rejection alone, but also upon his recognition and need to accept the basic bond between the parents and the discrepancy between the generations. He can enter into a latency period when he has fitted himself into a relatively conflict-free place in the family and established his position in relation to his parents. When he can identify with his family as a unit and feel secure in his dependency upon it, he can venture into the broader world with energies available to form new relationships and to invest in learning.

In our studies (Fleck, Lidz et al., 1957), we have noted the central moment of incestuous impulses in schizophrenic patients, and our studies of their families revealed that these were not simply regressive symptoms of the patient, but that one or both parents was also caught in incestuous ties to the patient—as in the case of Mr. N. who slept with his adolescent daughter for his needs as much as for hers; or of a mother, an amateur artist, who finds her painting of a mother caring for her sick son inadvertently turning into a painting of a mother having intercourse with her son; or another mother who tells us that we must cure her son, saying, "He is not just part of my life, he is all of my life. When he started to become sick I slept with him just like man and wife." There is a reciprocity to these impulses of the patients that provoke panic lest loss of their own self-control might lead to actual incest.

Such incestuous tendencies are a result of faulty family structure. In failing to provide an environment that precludes the arousal of conscious incestuous interests, the family fails in a fundamental requisite. The progression of the erotically toned child-parent attachment to an incestuous bond threatens the existence of the nuclear family, prevents the child from investing energies into extrafamilial socializing channels, and blocks his emergence as an adult. The prevention of incest, however, does not ordinarily rest upon conscious evocation of this universal taboo. The maintenance of a proper family structure normally keeps incestuous trends from becoming conscious or remaining conscious in adolescence. If conscious avoidance of incest becomes necessary because of defective family structure and role confusion, the personalities of family members become further distorted because spontaneous interaction becomes impossible, role conflict inevitable, and crippling defenses necessary.

I have sought to show that a firm parental coalition serves to prevent disruption of the generation boundaries within the family and the continuation of erotic bonds to a parent into adolescence. A parent who turns to a child for gratification of his emotional needs instead of to his spouse or extramaritally, moves the child across the generation boundaries; or when a child because of the schism between the parents can move into the breach, and replace one parent in satisfying the needs of the other, it becomes difficult to repress the oedipal erotic fantasies. Similarly, when gender roles are not properly maintained by parents, as when the father is weak and ineffectual or a masculine mother denies affection to her husband, the child can feel the lack and seek to assume the empty role. When the parents are united as parents and complementing each other's gender role, the child does not have the opportunity to fill an empty place in the wrong generation, but naturally grows to fill the proper position—as a childhood member of his or her sex.

I have specifically considered the relationship of the marital interaction of the parents, and the organization of the family they create, to the resolution of the child's oedipal situation because it is at this period that the ego structure and the internal directives of the superego begin to solidify—and an initial pattern for the later resolution of adolescent problems develops. I believe, however, that the parental interaction has a similar pervasive influence upon both earlier and later developmental phases. I also hope that it is clear that, although I have utilized illustrations from families with schizophrenic offspring, the same types of family problems, though usually less flagrant, initiate the faulty resolution of the oedipal conflict commonly encountered in the various neuroses.

I have not completed the survey of the requisites a marital relationship must fill to provide a proper milieu for rearing children. In the next lecture, I shall consider the need to provide an environment that transmits instrumentally useful ways of adaptation, particularly ways of communicating and thinking, suited to the culture in which the child will live.

SUMMARY

I have sought to focus attention on the importance of the marital interaction of parents upon the personality development of their children. The family, particularly when it exists as a relatively isolated nuclear family of parents and their children, gains structure from the interaction of the two parental personalities. The latter carry with them into the marriage their cultural backgrounds and the results of their experiences in their own parental families, and seek completion with the spouse in a family social system appropriate to and sanctioned by the society in which they live. While spouses can establish a great variety of relationships that may be satisfactory to them, the harmonious development of children requires certain essentials in the family organization. To provide this pattern, the parents must form a coalition as members of the parental generation, maintain appropriate sex-linked roles, and be capable of transmitting instrumentally useful ways of adaptation suited to the society in which the family exists. I have indicated some of the impediments to integrated personality development in the offspring when these few conditions cannot be achieved by the parents.

The approach that I have taken considers personality development from the perspective of the family matrix, considering the child as a member of a group entity in which the behavior of one member affects all. The family is recognized as a biologically required social institution that mediates between the biological and cultural directives of personality formation, and a social system in which the child assimilates the basic instrumentalities, institutions, and role attributions that are essential to his adaptation and integration.

I believe that viewing the problem of personality development according to such parameters, as well as according to how the child's needs are met at the various developmental phases, leads to some new insights, particularly concerning the continuing influence of the family environment through the years. Further, it affords a means of grasping the salient aspects of family life to compare from family to family, from culture to culture, and perhaps eventually to permit us to isolate features of family structure and interaction germane to the various personality disorders.

The Family, Language, and
Ego Functions

THE ADAPTIVE techniques that the child must acquire before he becomes reasonably self-sufficient are legion. I shall not endeavor to encompass the vast topic of the family's role in the enculturation of its children, but rather to consider a single aspect of it—the transmission of language and meanings—selected not as an illustrative example but because the totality of the process of enculturation depends upon it.

I

In the first of these three lectures, I emphasized that the uniquely human techniques of adaptation depended upon the evolution of a brain and neuromuscular system that permitted the use of tools and the development of that "tool of tools"—the word (Dewey, 1929). Through linguistic communication, man transmitted the fruits of experience from generation to generation, gradually accumulating and institutionalizing techniques of coping with the environment and for living together that each child must acquire. Even as the fetus recapitulates the genetic evolution of the species, following emergence from the womb, the child must assimilate an organized filtrate of the learning experiences of his forbears as they evolved into the institutions of his culture. Further, in order to adapt to new situations and conditions, and, indeed, to direct his life into the future, he must acquire the verbal tools that permit him to build up an internalized, symbolic representation of his world which he manipulates in imaginative trial and error before committing himself to irrevocable action. Although thinking utilizes visual symbols and other sensory modalities as well as words, language permits the selective recall of experiences and enables a person to draw converging lines into a hypothesized future toward which he can strive. The orientation toward future goals furthers survival through preparation in advance for contingencies and by releasing from a bondage to direct drive impulsion. Although a great deal more goes into ego functioning, without the capacities derived from language there cannot be any true ego at all.

As the ability to acquire language is an innate endowment of man, and because virtually all intact children learn to speak, we tend to take language very much for granted. We are apt to consider that the child learns the language in which he is reared and gains increasing facility to express himself in it and think with it as his central nervous system matures. Which language the child learns seems relatively unimportant; each provides a means of expressing his needs and thoughts. It required the linguistic and cultural investigations of Sapir (1949) and Whorf (1956) to shake these common-sense assumptions by providing evidence that the language which we learn profoundly influences the ways in which we perceive and experience. The language is an inherent part of the culture and in itself forms a major determinant of how a person thinks. It permits and delimits the way in which one thinks so completely, that one can scarcely grasp that persons raised in other cultures have very different, but equally valid, ways of experiencing and of thinking according to other systems of logic.

The ease with which we shift from one language to another to express the same concepts leads us to believe that languages are reasonably equivalent instruments of thought. Some annoying but trivial differences are apparent; e.g., "love" and *"amour"* are not identical, nor are *"mañana"* and "tomorrow." We become aggravated with foreigners who cannot properly grasp the meaning of such words as "democracy" and "freedom," no matter how carefully they are translated. We may consider that a major difference between German and English philosophy involves linguistic usage, for the German language permits the invention of new words to express illusory, subjective, and rather vague concepts—a tendency that has reached its apotheosis in Heidegger's work (1929). English demands the fitting of new concepts into the existing vocabulary. The German can be master of the language, whereas the Englishman must master the language. We are, however, usually comparing Indo-European tongues, most of which had a common origin and are expressions of cultures that have intercommunicated and influenced each other. When we seek to understand and translate languages of cultures that developed along very different lines since the earliest days of man, such as the Amerindian tongues, Hopi, Shawnee, and Navajo, the situation is vastly different.

These languages are not so readily translatable into English because each expresses a different way of categorizing and thinking about the environment and experiences. The study of such cultures and their languages broadens our horizons and leads to the realization that people are directed by their language to classify things and events according to the words provided, and that their thinking is influenced profoundly by the way in which the language is put together syntactically. The Hopi, for example, live in a relatively timeless world, or at least have a very different concept of time, and their verbs have no tenses (Whorf, 1940, 1941a, 1941b, 1942). As they lead a relatively static existence and live in a very small area, their entire conceptualization of experience differs from ours, so that they manage very well without an arbitrary present separating a past from an imagined future. To the Hopi (perhaps not unlike Samuel Butler's [1927] Erewhonians who followed determinism to its radical conclusion) everything already exists, and they divide events into those which have become manifest and those which are in the process of becoming but are not yet manifest. If I grasp correctly what Whorf writes, events in different localities are not on the same time scale, for there is no such metaphorical unrolling of time on space. The "not yet manifest" is not, as we might at first think, equivalent to a future, but applies also to subjective thoughts. In a sense, it is true enough that the future is also known to us only as a subjective expectation. The Hopi consider thinking and concentration to be a means of bringing about manifestation. In a ritual, collective concentration brings rain or influences the corn to grow; and illness results from malevolent thoughts of others, or from the sick person's own thoughts. The Hopi verbs are also modified to indicate how something is known to the speaker—through seeing it, by report, because it is a rule, etc.—and the Hopi may be puzzled how we can manage without such verb forms. We might also note that time is not divided into a sequence of days, but rather "day" returns in the sense of the same person returning after an absence. In a related way, the Hopi do not arbitrarily disrupt the continuity of nature by having such discrete entities as a "hill," but have a place where the ground rises; nor do they perceive the non-existent entity of a "wave," but the water making a slosh or undulating.

Languages like Shawnee use an entirely different approach, fusing an entire concept or sentence into a single word by using symbols that combine in manifold ways to elicit an appropriate image. The widely held notion that such languages are primitive and concrete because these people cannot think abstractly is untenable, for as Whorf has demonstrated, they are far more abstract than European languages in many ways. They convey different ways of conceiving that we cannot grasp readily, just as those of us educated to follow the axioms and logic of Euclid have difficulties in grasping the equally valid systems of non-Euclidian geometries that are often more useful.

Although the ability to use language is an inherent attribute, the language which any person uses and the way in which he thinks through using it depend upon where and how he is brought up. Peoples everywhere, however, must cope with problems that are virtually identical because of their common biological endowment and the identities in their environments. Therefore they designate and communicate about many of the same things which provide common reference points between divergent cultures and their languages. Still the division of the environment into categories varies widely, and ways of thinking even more widely. The language constitutes a type of social contract unwittingly imposed upon the members of a culture. They are, as Whorf (1941a) points out, "parties to an agreement to organize it in this way . . . and its terms are absolutely obligatory . . . for they cannot talk at all except by subscribing to the organization and classification of data which the agreement decrees." How does a child become a participant in this contract? How certain is he to learn its terms? What happens if he fails to learn them properly? These are questions that I wish to explore, focusing particularly upon how the child learns to categorize experiences through gaining the meanings of words—a requisite for communicating and self-direction and thereby to the understanding of ego functions. Such questions lead to consideration of the family's role in teaching language and meanings—and eventually to a way of studying the deviances in conceptual thinking that form the core problem of schizophrenia.

Let us consider the categorizing function of words. In learning words, the child acquires a system of dividing the ceaseless flow of his experiences into categories that enables him to communicate about them. The vocabulary of the language provides a reference system of the ways in which the culture categorizes. The Navajo do not make a distinction between grey and brown; and some African tribes have no names by which they can refer to colors. We may find it odd that the Eskimos have no generic word for snow or the Hopi no inclusive word for corn, upon which their subsistence rests. However, we scarcely note that we must use a cumbersome expression such as "writing instruments" to refer to pens, pencils, crayons and typewriters as a unit, and that we have no expression that covers nails, tacks, screws, and staples. If the vocabulary were not available, the child would have the impossible task of starting from scratch to divide up his environment into useful categories, and if it were possible, he would arrive at a very different set of categories.

Categories are formed by selecting out common attributes of things or events to bestow some degree of equivalence to them: chairs can be sat upon, ceilings are the covering partitions of rooms, etc. Each thing or event can be categorized in a multiplicity of ways according to the attributes utilized; e.g., a squash ball can be grouped with objects that are "round," or with rubber objects, with black objects, or with "balls." One factor in intelligence depends upon the ability to categorize the same experience in many ways—to understand its relationships to a variety of events. To a very great extent, such capacities depend upon having available the words that designate the categories and the meanings of these categories.

It is only by means of categorizing through abstracting common attributes that communicating about events is possible. Without categorizing, we could only appreciate each individual object or event as an isolated and never-recurring experience. Valid communication would scarcely be possible and little could be learned from experiences. Roger Brown (1958) has pointed out that if we understand history to be the stream of events appreciated in all of their particulars, the study of history cannot provide lessons for the future, for there can never be recurrences; but if attributes are abstracted from historical events, we will find that history recurs in certain essentials. The same considerations apply to the possibility of learning from life experiences: unless we categorize them we cannot compare and form expectations. Herein lies a vital characteristic of words—their meanings provide us with a set of expectancies that make reflective thinking possible. Words have a predictive value that permits utilization of experience and thus they are fundamental to ego functions. I shall elaborate on this critical quality of words and meanings.

Let us assume that I am holding a pencil. It can be categorized in various ways according to the characteristics selected: it is yellow, wooden, hexagonal, an elongated pointed object, a phallic symbol, etc. Each grouping is appropriate in the proper context and conveys a prediction; i.e., it absorbs colors of certain wave lengths; it can be whittled; it will fit into a six-sided hole, etc. However, a child who is unfamiliar with pencils would not group my pencil with others of different shapes, sizes, materials, colors. He would require considerable experimentation to learn its primary purpose rather than to consider it an object for throwing, breaking or poking. The name "pencil," however, neglects all of the incidental attributes to focus on the critical attribute of "containing graphite in a form usable for marking on paper." This is the meaning of "pencil." While intelligent behavior relates to the ability to include the object in a variety of categories, it also depends upon the ability to determine the critical attributes designated by a name (Bruner et al., 1956). If the child knows that names designate categories (as he learns very early in life without realizing it), he anticipates that the word "pencil" refers to a class of objects with some distinctive characteristic. He asks what a pencil is, or what it is for. When he is shown or told, he is led to an expectation that serves to guide future behavior. He expects to be able to write with a pencil regardless of its size, shape, color, or material, even though he has only seen yellow wooden pencils. Without this predictive value of words contained in their categorizing function, experiences would be disorganized and existence far more aleatory. From the many attributes of a pencil, the name categorizes according to the attributes that permit its use for writing and carries the expectation that it can be so

[85]

utilized. A chair can be sat upon; a woman but not a man can become pregnant; pneumococcus pneumonia but not virus pneumonia will respond to penicillin, etc. The predictive value of words often provides direction and precludes the necessity for trial-and-error learning.

The trustworthiness of an expectancy produced by a word depends upon the ability to appreciate the critically defining attributes of the word. The understanding of "pencil" as "something that writes" is useful but imprecise. If a child who had learned to erase is given a pen instead of a pencil, his expectations of erasability will be frustrated. If "mother" means "a married woman with nurturant feelings toward her children," even though the definition may often be useful, the word can arouse erroneous expectations that a more critical definition, "a female parent," would avoid. I might observe, perhaps somewhat gratuitously, that we are not very intelligent about "schizophrenia" because we are unable to know definitively the critical attributes of this categorization.

The categorizing of experiences through the abstraction of common attributes, the labeling of categories by words, and the attainment of meanings of words by defining the critical attributes designated by the word are essential to ego development and to ego functioning. The infant is not born, strictly speaking, adapted to survive in an average expectable environment as Hartmann has stated (1958). Rather, in order to survive, each society has developed a set of institutions that take infants' essential needs into

[86]

account. Through the use of linguistic tools, the child learns the culture's institutions and techniques of adaptation more or less adequately, and he gains an ability to delay the gratification of basic drives, to internalize parental attributes, directives, and teachings, to consider group needs as well as his own, and to be motivated by future security as well as by drive impulsion. Through the categories provided by language, the world in which he lives, his own needs, and the behavior of others gain some degree of order and predictability.

The meanings of words, which are so important to human development and survival are, as we have seen, not something inherent in the words themselves nor established by some logic determined by the way the brain functions or nature is constituted. The learning of critical attributes requires time and experience. What the child means by "a mother" is very different from what the word means to him as a behavioral scientist thirty years later. Indeed, the words uttered when first used in early childhood are but empty shells relatively devoid of meaning. They require both delimitation and expansion to attain usefulness: the word "water," for example, may originally be used for both the fluid and the glass and spread to designate many fluids and various shiny objects before it is progressively constricted and defined; on the other hand, the meaning of the word expands with the increasing variety of experiences with water. Many aspects of studies of the development of the ability to conceptualize, categorize, and think "abstractly" are, in essence, studies of the development of meanings. It is apparent that the acquisition of meanings is not dependent upon physical maturation alone, but also upon the nature and breadth of the child's experiences.

There are, then, two aspects to the development of meanings: the learning of the words of the culture's language and their shared meanings; and the gradual and continuing development of personal meanings of words through the individual's idiosyncratic experiences with the symbol and with what it denotes. Reasonable accuracy in the knowledge and use of the shared meanings forms the basis of linguistic communication, obligatory for participation in social interaction and for learning other instrumentalities of the culture. The personal meaning of a word should properly develop in accordance with the shared dictionary meaning, but confusions and even contradictions inevitably arise, creating difficulties in both communicating and thinking.

Now, this vocabulary and its meanings, together with how the words are joined syntactically to enable communication, are taught the child by his elders and to a very great extent by members of his family. The subtle and highly involved process is carried out largely unwittingly and is subject to many unconscious influences. The child uses words to attempt to solve problems. Stated simply, meanings are established rapidly or slowly, with certainty or uncertainty according to how effectively and consistently proper usage attains objectives for the child (Mark, 1962). The process depends upon reciprocal interaction between the child and his tutors; the consistency between the teachers; the cues they provide; the sounds to which they respond or remain oblivious; the meanings which they reward consistently or sporadically or indicate are useless, ineffectual, undesirable, repugnant, or punishable. Still other factors are involved in the attainment of communicative meanings, some of which I shall touch upon.

The personal meanings of words differ for each person because they are composites of the individual's experiences with each word and with what it symbolizes. The word is a symbolic focal point from which the various associations connected with it radiate. It forms an entrance point for the recall of these experiences. It also forms an abstraction of the common attributes of the things that the word classifies. It provides a way of indicating or thinking about the topic subsumed under the heading of the word without entering upon separate associations—the carrier of a mental set, emotional intonations, and unconscious connotations. The word "dog" may have first meant for a child the stuffed animal that served as a transitional object; later, the single household pet; and eventually, an expanding number of dogs encountered under differing circumstances. The meaning of "dog" will include the mother's love or fear of dogs, and it will change if the person is bitten by a dog, etc. While such personal meanings change throughout life, the foundations of most basic words continue to carry elements of early childhood experiences. The meaning of "mother" can be rid only with difficulty, if at all, of feelings and expectations aroused in the child by his mother. "Being good" may carry

[89]

throughout life the implication of strict obedience, or of demonstrating affection to parents, or of not getting diry. Even though the shared or dictionary meaning is firmly established, as for example, "father" meaning "a male parent," the strictness, authority, or rivalry of the actual father, or his kindly attitudes contribute to defining "a male parent." A patient, to note one instance, more or less consciously categorized "mothers" and "crocodiles" together on the basis of the common attributes of devouring their young, shedding false tears, and castrating proclivities (the last item based upon a joke about a crocodile castrating a swimmer). To this man, teeth formed a critical attribute of mothers, and indeed of all women. The intrafamilial transactions influence personal meanings in many ways, including which associations intrude inappropriately, or which are repressed and influence unconsciously.

The child's experiences within his family, then, play a critical role in his acquisition of both culturally established communicative meanings and personal meanings. Do some children, because of the faulty transmission of meanings by their parents, fail to learn properly the culture's ways of categorizing and communicating and thus lack adequate means of relating to others, understanding their experiences, and attaining useful expectations? Or, do they develop aberrant and confused personal meanings that intrude upon and distort the shared meanings? Can improper learning of meanings limit adaptive capacities and cause a major impairment to ego functions? I have returned to the original question: Can major deficiencies in ego development and functioning relate to disturbances in the primary parental function of transmitting a cardinal instrumental technique to the next generation?

II

I have been examining the critical position of words and their meanings in human development and adaptation and have suggested that serious impairments of ego functioning may be related to failures of parents to transmit properly the culture's linguistic tools. Now, I wish to turn again to our studies of the intrafamilial environments in which schizophrenic patients grew up to examine clinical evidence for the feasibility of the hypothesis.

Although schizophrenia has eluded precise definition, the critical characteristics that distinguish this category of mental illness concern the disturbed symbolic processes without degradation of intelligence potential.* The core problem has been designated in various ways that involve related capacities: disordered concept formation, concretistic thinking, mislabeled metaphor, impaired categorical thinking, in-

* The thought disorder in schizophrenia differs from the disorders created by any known type of brain damage or toxic disorder affecting the central nervous system. The thought disturbances accompanying temporal lobe epilepsy may resemble schizophrenic thinking most closely, but are distinguishable by mental tests (Schafer and Glaser, 1963). Even chronic schizophrenic patients may carry out highly complex intellectual tasks. A young man learns analytic geometry; another is capable of analyzing the stock market perspicaciously; another composes intricate music. August Strindberg, though artistically sterile when most disturbed, wrote many of his plays while clearly schizophrenic and actively delusional.

trusions of primary process material, derailment of associations, etc. The thought disorder has led countless investigators to search for a metabolic or anatomical cause of a hypothesized brain dysfunction in schizophrenia. Even Vygotsky (1934), who pointed out the imperative need for studies of the development of the conceptual disorders in schizophrenic patients and laid the foundations for such studies, considered the schizophrenic difficulties to be secondary to disordered cerebral functioning. However, as I have been indicating, failures to attain or maintain valid meanings will inevitably result in disturbances in conceptual thinking. Norman Cameron (1938), following his classic studies of schizophrenic thinking, concluded that the conceptual distortions arise secondarily to the patient's withdrawal from social interaction. My colleagues and I have suggested that, confronted by an untenable conflict and unable to find a path into the future, the schizophrenic patient withdraws from the demands of society and reality by breaking the confines imposed by the meanings and logic of his culture which, in turn, further isolates the patient (Lidz, Cornelison et al., 1958b). The condition tends to become self-perpetuating because the patient ceases to test the instrumental utility of his concepts and no longer seeks the consensus of meanings required for living cooperatively with others. A theory of schizophrenia, however, needs to explain not only a person's needs to abandon consensual meanings and reality testing, but also why it is possible for him to do so whereas others in similar dilemmas cannot. As the attainment of a firm and useful system of meanings appears to depend upon a number of factors in the developmental process, and because evidence was accumulating that schizophrenic persons are raised in seriously disturbed families by disturbed parents, we sought to ascertain if the patients had received a faulty grounding in learning the shared meanings of the culture within their families. If adaptive capacities depend upon the assimilation of the meanings of the culture—its way of categorizing—such persons would encounter serious difficulties in understanding and coping with life experiences and in forming nondependent relationships; and they would be more prone to distort meanings to suit needs and wishes than persons in whom the culture's meaning system had been firmly established.

When we turned to the families with schizophrenic offspring that we had studied intensively to focus specifically upon the rationality of the parents and the nature of the intrafamilial communications, we found that all of our patients had persistently been exposed to distortions of meanings and paralogical reasoning that would almost have precluded attainment of a firm foundation in reality testing. We reported only the gross and rather obvious distorting influences because the severity of the disturbances eclipsed the more subtle influences. Let me review briefly the findings we reported.

Even though none of the parents had ever been hospitalized for a mental disorder, over sixty per cent of the patients had at least one parent who was either schizophrenic or paranoid. The situation was particularly deleterious because this parent's strange ways and ideas were scarcely countered by the spouse who either accepted or became resigned to them, or withdrew from the family situation. How serious were these influences? I shall illustrate briefly.

A young man with long hair and flowing beard, clad only in his shorts, sits reading *The Wall Street Journal*. He believes himself a reincarnation of the Buddha. In his home, his father who had been a highly successful business man, had spent much of his time isolated in his bedroom reading either Eastern theology or stock market bulletins. A member of an esoteric cult, the father had considered himself the reincarnation of an Asiatic divinity, a belief his wife and the governess shared and taught the children. How deeply did the teachings penetrate? The patient's sister had become a successful commercial artist, aided by many years of intensive psychotherapy. When asked if much of the patient's behavior were not an expression of their father's ideas, the sister blanched and exclaimed, "The poor boy—he is so right!"

Another bearded youth wore trousers but no shoes. When he was born his mother had confided to her diary her hopes that she had given birth to the Messiah and for years recorded the family life in idealized terms that bore little resemblance to the unhappy reality. As the years passed, the mother became increasingly delusional, conveying her persecutory fears to her children and often acting at the direction of hallucinated voices. The father who had left the home when the patient was young had never recognized that his wife was mentally ill.

In another family, the mother supports the household for the father had been incapacitated by a "nervous breakdown" shortly after the patient's birth. He admonishes his sons to cleave to the advice and direction of their mother who, despite her business competence, has been actively delusional for many years believing her telephone to be "tapped" and that neighbors might burn down the home. The father of a young woman believes in a world conspiracy of Catholics and constantly warns of malevolence of Catholics, a situation that created much confusion as his wife was a devout Catholic. The patient had become the focal point in the controversy that had started prior to her conception and involved every phase of her upbringing.

While such findings can be considered as evidence of a genetic transmission of schizophrenia, the aberrant parental behavior chronically influenced the children's conceptualizations and the meanings learned in these families.

The study of the influences of these schizophrenic or paranoid parents led to some generalizations that applied to families with less overtly disturbed parents. The parents can maintain their own integration only under sharply circumscribed conditions; their precarious equilibrium will topple unless the environment can be delimited, or if they must shift from the one role that they rigidly maintain and which the family must support. Reality cannot alter nor new circumstances modify the conception of themselves and the family that they must hold. They perceive and act in accordance with these needed preconceptions, relinquishing them only under extreme pressures. Then they manage to explain away through projection or they use the mechanism of isolation to ward off the impact. The parents' delimitation of the environment and their alteration of perceptions and meanings create a strange family milieu filled with inconsistencies, contradictory meanings, and denial of what should be obvious. Facts are constantly being altered to suit emotionally determined needs. The children who must subjugate their own needs to the parents' defenses also learn that meanings are not primarily in the service of reality testing. Their conceptualizations of experiences are instrumental in helping solve parental problems rather than in mastering events and feelings, nor are they in accord with what children in other families experience. The acceptance of mutually contradictory experiences requires paralogical thinking. Such environments provide training in irrationality.

Several phenomena commonly observed in families of schizophrenic patients follow as corollaries upon the parents' inabilities to perceive, understand, or tolerate anything that does not fit into their own rigid defenses. "Impervious" is a term frequently applied to mothers or fathers of schizophrenic patients, indicating their inability to perceive the child's emotional needs. The parent may listen but does not hear what the child says, and is even more oblivious to unspoken cues. It is a characteristic that conveys an uncanny impression, particularly when combined with the inordinate intrusiveness into the child's life by which such parents seek to control and delimit to maintain their own defenses. A mother is unaware of the agony she causes her son by repeated complaints to his teachers of their failure to recognize his genius and because they do not correct his schoolmates' neglect of him. Another mother takes over the class from an astounded teacher to demonstrate how her child can better be included in class activities. In a family group therapy session, a hebephrenic college girl finally manages to pour out her feelings of desperate loneliness in her family and her hopelessness about gaining affection and guidance from her parents; as she pleads with them, her mother turns to the therapist and remarks casually, "My dress is getting tight. I suppose I should diet." The mother was falling back on her habitual pattern of blocking out anything that might upset her equanimity.

Some of these parents appear to devote themselves inordinately to the child, but they are responding primarily to their own needs, wishes, and feelings as projected onto the child, as when a mother feeds a child because she herself is hungry, or gives a laxative when she is constipated. More commonly, a parent intrudes into doing the child's schoolwork, choice of friends, selection of an adult offspring's clothes, etc., controlling and intruding to maintain the parent's security operations. The parent, usually the mother, cannot establish ego boundaries between herself and the child, and continues to treat the child as an extension of herself, using him to complete her own life. Such parents in responding to their own needs rather than the child's are oblivious to the child's cues and can produce drastic confusion concerning signals of physiological motivation and the learning of self-direction, as well as of the meanings of signs in general, creating a despair over the usefulness and validity of communication.

"Masking" is another common consequence of parents' needs to maintain the necessary image of themselves and their family. Some extremely disturbing situation within the family is denied or ignored and family members are expected to behave as if it did not exist. A parent who cannot accept a family situation that would upset his emotional equilibrium acts and communicates as if the family were a harmonious unit filling the needs of its members. The children are aware that something is amiss, but learn that questions must not be asked and many things must not be mentioned. They learn to ignore the obvious and that a major use of words is to explain away what cannot be changed. Although some "masking" probably occurs in all families, in most of the families of schizophrenic patients the masking affected the entire interaction. The father of two late adolescent children had been absent from the home for many years, supposedly because the pursuit of a series of paranoid lawsuits kept him in another city. He wrote each week that he would soon return but never appeared, and the mother kept insisting to the children that nothing was wrong with her marriage, always reassuring them that their father would be home again within a week. Another woman not only supported the family for more than a decade after her husband suffered a serious reverse in his career, but also maintained her husband's professional office to pretend to the world, to herself, and to the children that her husband was still an eminent man. Under such conditions, a very large segment of the communication within the family must be distorted and unreal, and the children learn to distrust their own perceptions and what words mean.

In some of these families the children were consciously trained to a paranoid orientation. The children were taught a parent's persecutory ideas that neighbors were inimical or dangerous, or that anything outsiders or relatives learned about the family would be used against them. In some, people were divided into two categories, members of the immediate family and outsiders, and an attribute of outsiders was "inimicable." Even more disturbing in a few families was the inculcation of a paranoid distrust of one parent by the other, or of all persons of the opposite sex from the paranoid parent.

This first survey of the rationality of the communications within families in which schizophrenic patients had grown up only sought to provide a general assessment. It revealed that serious distorting influences had existed in all of the families throughout, or almost throughout, the patients' lives. These influences educated to aberrant ways of thinking and provided a faulty grounding in the meanings of experiences and of the words that designated them. The study suggested how irrationalities of parents and of parental relationships can be transmitted to children and become more pervasive and disorganizing in the children. It indicated an area that requires intensive investigation. Studies in progress which compare the projective tests and tests of categorical thinking of schizophrenic patients and their parents indicate clearly that the patients' conceptual disorders do not arise *de novo* out of their own life problems, but have precursors in the perception and think-ing of the parents who raised them and provided most of their early education in problem-solving and lin-guistic usage (Lidz, Wild et al, 1962; and Singer).

Other contemporaneous investigations into the na-ture and etiology of schizophrenia have reached closely related findings concerning the influences of faulty parent-child communication. Bateson, Jack-son, et al. (1956) have elaborated a communicational theory of the etiology of schizophrenia, their "double-bind" hypothesis. Essentially, the hypothesis assumes that what occurs within a narrow context will be affected by the wider context and that there can be conflict between the context and metacontext. "The person is then faced with the dilemma either of being wrong in the primary context, or of being right for the wrong reasons or in the wrong way." They con-sider "the hypothesis that schizophrenic communica-tion is learned and becomes habitual as a result of continual traumata of this kind" (Bateson, 1960). Their studies had led to a concern with the faulty learning of meanings in the family setting and they hypothesize that the schizophrenic patient "must live in a universe where the sequence of events is such that his unconventional communicational habits will be in some sense appropriate" (Bateson, Jackson et al., 1956).

Hilde Bruch has taken a different though related approach to elucidating the genesis of perceptual and conceptual confusions in schizophrenic patients. She noted the inability of patients with anorexia nervosa and some obese persons to recognize physiological signals of hunger or satiety, confusing such signals with those of anxiety or of emotional emptiness. She found that their own inner awareness had "not been programmed correctly" (Bruch, 1961; Bruch and Palombo, 1961). To take a simple example, an obese youth may have had little opportunity to learn properly to relate sensations of hunger to the need for food because from early infancy his mother had responded to any cry or restlessness by stuffing a bottle into his mouth and continued to misinterpret any of his cues or complaints of discontent as evidence of a need for food. Bruch points out that it is erroneous to assume that the human organism "knows" its bodily sensations and the nature of its drives. Recognition of bodily needs and the behavior appropriate for satisfying them depends upon learning starting in infancy. Similar defects in programming occur in schizophrenic development concerning physiological needs, the definition of ego boundaries, the reinforcement of behavioral patterns, and the meanings of experiences which seriously impair and confuse efforts at problem solving and the attainment of a sense of autonomy and capacity for initiative.

The examination of the family milieu of schizophrenic patients reveals that the patients were habitually exposed to concepts and meanings deviant from the shared communicative meanings of the culture and to influences that would adversely affect the development of consistent and coherent personal meanings. Flaws in adaptive capacities related to defective categorizing and to confusions of meanings are also inherent in other personality disturbances such as the neuroses and psychopathies. All mechanisms of defense are means of altering the perception or meaning of experiences to make them more tenable and less anxiety-provoking.

III

The attainment of instrumentally useful meanings is essential to mature adaptation, and I wish to examine some of the ways in which the parent-child transactions influence linguistic development. Although Piaget, Vygotsky, and others have studied the lengthy process by which a child gains the capacity to form mature concepts and think logically—studies which belatedly are beginning to influence psychiatric thinking about ego functioning—such studies of the maturation of the thought processes are incomplete when separated from the remainder of personality development (Inhelder and Piaget, 1958; Piaget, 1956, 1928; Vygotsky, 1962). As the studies of the schizophrenic patients show, the development of meanings cannot properly be considered separately from the influences of family organization upon ego structure, nor from other interpersonal transactions within the family. I shall seek only to indicate some of the areas that require study and to stimulate interest in an orientation that may clarify some critical problems concerning ego functions.

The ways in which deficiencies of parental guidance can adversely influence the child's linguistic development will be discussed under two general headings: (1) the inadequate stimulation or actual discouragement of language development, and (2) the inculcation of aberrant or confused meanings.

The foundations for language development are established during the preverbal period of infancy. The nurturant person's responsivity to the child's needs and spontaneous activities creates an expectation of understanding in the child. The child starts to learn meanings prior to using words through responding to maternal cues and through the responses of others to the indefinite cues he provides. Meanings are established because they help solve problems. The parents' efforts to alleviate the child's needs and to obtain relief from the discomfort that his crying arouses in them are guided by only very diffuse signals. Some parents, because of their greater experience, empathy, intelligence or attention, successfully assuage the infant's needs more consistently than others. The babies of those who chronically misinterpret will gain little experience in solving problems through providing signals.

Virtually every child starts to babble spontaneously, but the continuation and elaboration of the babbling requires responsivity from others. The hearing of language directs a drift to the vocalization of the sounds used by the culture's language and, later, to utterances and words that elicit specific responses (McCarthy, 1930). Deaf children who cannot hear themselves or others cease to babble. Children raised in institutions that provide only routinized care lag in their speech and intellectual development which may result from the linguistic vacuum in which they are raised as well as from the deprivation of maternal nurturance. Raising a child in the parental home rather than an orphanage does not provide assurance of adequate verbal stimulation. In studying schizophrenic patients, a history is often obtained of meager cathexis of the baby by the mother because of her preoccupations, apathy, depression, or anxiety.

The child's attainment of the ability to understand and use words greatly facilitates the collaboration required to care for the child's needs. The rapidity and firmness with which meanings are established depend upon the consistency with which the tutors use words and respond to the child's words. The greater the consistency with which a word solves a problem, the more firmly the connection becomes automatized, diminishing the need to search for ways of obtaining a solution and releasing energy and attention for other purposes. The learning of meanings depends upon interpersonal interaction. Each time the word elicits a similar and appropriate response, its meaning is both delimited and expanded. As has been noted, the word "water" may at first be used to designate objects that appear with the water, and even for objects that resemble the glass in some attribute such as shininess; but a reasonably consistent arrival of water that assuages thirst establishes one firm meaning for the word—a connection that provides a simple and economical means of relieving thirst and defining thirst. Thirst need no longer produce a random searching either mentally or behaviorally that preempts attention. However, should the word "water" produce a diversity of responses—water, milk, candy, cuddling, being taken to urinate, being taken into mother's bed, scolding—it may take a long time to relate the word to the fluid. It may, perhaps, simply become a means of obtaining attention. Undue delay in the automatization of the basic meaning may permit continued intrusions of inappropriate associations, including intrusions of primary process material out of context. "Water" may continue to evoke feelings of sleeping with mother or retain a firm connection with urine. Such situations commonly exist concerning sexual drives because of the blocks placed in the way of the child's learning to recognize sexual feelings and solving problems aroused by them.

Interference with a child's efforts to explore his world and solve problems by himself can also impede language development. If the child is treated as a passive object for whom everything must be done, as often happens with a mother who cannot let the child differentiate from her, the need to speak and to learn meanings is minimized. A related consideration concerns verbal play. Even as the child gains mastery of his bodily movements and learns to measure space with the help of countless playful explorations, he tries out words and expressions in a multitude of contexts and learns from the responses elicited. He repeats what the parent says and does, often imaginatively exchanging roles with a parent. "You are thirsty, mommy, you cry for water, here is water." The child learns the reciprocal role, a part of the process of identification, and expands his comprehension and use of words. Parents who need to adhere firmly to reality and cannot permit such play with meanings discourage such exploratory problem solving.

The development of trust in the utility and validity of verbal communication forms a critical step in development that has received little attention. Can words help solve problems? Do they promote collaborative interaction? Do they help increase predictability or obfuscate? Do they help achieve satisfaction in reality or simply provide a means of fantasied gratification? Failures or deficiencies in inculcating trust in language both discourage linguistic development and produce confusions of meanings.

The child's trust in verbal communication depends upon whether the words of the essential nurturant persons help him solve problems or confuse, whether they provide more consistent signals than nonverbal cues, and whether the child's use of words can evoke desired responses. Difficulties arise, for example, when a parent's words contradict nonverbal signals, as when a mother's irritable and hostile handling of the child is accompanied by words of affection, or when a parent's pleasure in the child's destructiveness or mischievousness negates the reprimands. The value of words will be doubted if erroneous solutions are habitually imposed, as when a child who complains that he is hungry is told that he is tired and must go to bed. The predictive usages of communications will not be trusted if promises rarely materialize. "Eat and I'll read you a story," the child is told, but after he has eaten there is "no time for a story." A schizophrenic youth recalled vividly how he had not only learned to distrust his mother's promises but also to cease listening to her constant talk, for he had learned very early that her tales of the wonderful things they would do on the morrow never materialized. Not until many years later did he realize that his mother was simply verbalizing the fantasies that sustained her.

Persistent denial of the correctness of the child's perceptions can have a particularly malignant influence in fostering distrust of language and in teaching distorted meanings. As noted in the discussion of the families of schizophrenic patients, such conditions habitually arise with parents who must maintain their own version of events to preserve their precarious equilibrium. The child is repeatedly placed in a "bind" because the obvious is negated and he is threatened with punishment or loss of love if he does not see things as the parent requires. Signals become unpredictable and the child learns to ignore his perceptions or to bestow upon words a magical capacity to obliterate feelings and occurrences. A simple example can be cited from a family group therapy session. The schizophrenic daughter who was trying to begin to express her feelings commented that a visit home had been marred by her father's nagging. The mother instantaneously responded, "Your father never nags," even though the father had been nagging his daughter earlier in the session. A few minutes later the patient confided in her mother, "I find that I'm often uneasy with you," which brought the reply, "If you are, you're the only person who is." Yet, the hospital personnel all found it difficult to be at ease with this woman.

Parents can impede language development in numerous ways, but the illustrations should suffice to indicate how they can fail to cultivate and guide the child's innate predisposition, and convey how intimately the process is bound up with the totality of the parent-child transactions.

Although I noted some of the ways in which families can inculcate deviant meanings and distorted ways of conceptualizing in discussing the transmission of irrationality in schizophrenic families, the process requires further comment.

In all families some words have meanings that are idiosyncratic to the family and obscure to outsiders. The connotations of words differ from family to family, but usually the conventional communicative meanings are also used and recognized. However, consistent deviant usage of words by nurturant figures leaves a child poorly prepared for communicating outside the home. It is unusual for simply designatory meanings to be erroneous, "black" called "white" or "mother" called "father." The difficulties occur at higher levels—the learning to fill in correctly the category for which the word is a referent; to form proper superordinate and subordinate categories and to discriminate between them; to achieve meanings based upon critical attributes; to maintain discrete categories unencumbered by inappropriate intrusions; not to concretize metaphor; and other related disturbances. Still, for practical purposes even reversals of "black" and "white," and "mother" and "father" may be taught. I can recall the confusions that arose in the children of a colored woman with a white husband; she had always insisted that her daughters were not "black" but "white" in opposition to their own and the southern community's perceptions. The reversal clearly expanded to influence profoundly many other meanings the children were taught. In another family, the male parent who performs virtually all of the maternal and housewifely functions while his wife supports the family is properly called "father," but the set of expectations aroused by "mother" and "father" are deviant.

Faulty meanings of isolated words are in themselves relatively unimportant, but often they are indications of significant attitudes that influence broad areas of meanings, or are but part of the aberrant family milieu. The grouping of "play" with "sin" or "policeman" with "enemy" involves many meanings. A patient insisted that until he was adolescent he had believed that "constipation" meant "being angry with mother," for whenever he became angry with his mother, she said that he was constipated and gave him an enema. The enema was administered according to a seductive-aggressive ritual that could not but promote intrusions of erotic and sadistic associations into "defecation," and incestuous and phallic associations into the meanings of "mother" and "woman." As might be anticipated, this mother's behavior created distortions of meanings in many other areas as well.

Some meanings learned within the family reflect the family's religious, ethnic, and social class membership and create greater or lesser difficulties in communicating outside of the family. A family that is highly deviant from the societal matrix in which it exists can create almost insuperable problems for the children when they must emerge from the home. More commonly, conflicts between the meaning systems of two parents raised in different cultures or subcultures confuse the child's meanings. The differences between the parents' meanings and values may be overt as in the case of the devout Catholic mother who completely accepted the teachings of the Church and considered the priest as an authority superordinate to her husband, whereas her husband denounced all priests as scoundrels and the tenets of the Church as nonsense; or the differences may be covert as when a lower-class father defines a "good son" by expectations of toughness and sharpness in business while the mother from a higher social background expects a son to assume the academic standards of her father.

The effects of serious and habitual distortions of meanings and of paralogical thinking by parents who are mentally ill probably require no further amplification. However, there is a tendency to minimize how many children are exposed to such influences. Parents who are borderline schizophrenic or somewhat paranoid are not counted in the statistics of mental illness. A vague and rambling mother who is more or less schizophrenic may obscure meanings to an extent that even a psychiatrist has difficulty in communicating with her, but her children have been exposed to her blurrings and inconsistencies of meanings since they were born. A father who is only considered somewhat rigid and overbearing by his business colleagues, at home dominates the behavior and thinking of the family with his paranoid rigidity and distrust. Such circumstances are apt to be more malignant when the deviances are not sufficiently pronounced to be categorized as "crazy," or when the distortions of the disturbed parent are accepted by the other parent; or when the parent holds a place of esteem in the community and therefore must be right.

The parental function of transmitting valid linguistic instruments to their offspring cannot, of course, be sharply separated from the inculcation of other techniques essential for proper self-direction. Careful observation of schizophrenic patients in remission often reveals an amazing ignorance of simple skills. A highly intelligent young woman, who was a fine painter, had never learned to put her stockings on properly or how to buy and adjust a brassiere; neither had she ever shopped in a grocery store nor learned the rudiments of cooking. It is not essential for all women to know how to cook, but the meaning of a pork chop is limited if known only in the form served at the table. The lack of knowledge of how to dress clearly influences adaptive techniques. The same patient also displayed an ignorance of social amenities that bears a relationship to linguistic meanings. She had little understanding of such nonverbal cues as those indicating a polite or profound interest in her, or whether an invitation was perfunctory or serious. Actually the profound "masking" and disparity between verbal and nonverbal cues that existed in her family virtually prevented such learning. The way the patient behaved, including the way she dressed, provided cues that set up erroneous expectations just as much as if she had used the wrong words.

The nuclear family, shaped by the personalities of the parents and their ways of relating, is not the sole enculturating agency. As discussed in the first lecture, the influence of parents and their idiosyncracies are diluted in societies or segments of societies with extensive kinship systems. Although our contemporary industrialized society depends upon schools to transmit a large proportion of the knowledge required in a complex society, the foundations are established during the preschool years and largely at home. Peer groups also play a significant role in transmitting skills, mores and patterns required at each age. Premature substitution of peer group teaching for parental teaching may contribute to instability as noted in delinquent neighborhoods. On the other hand, a child's failure to associate with peer groups can act to preserve the eccentric and idiosyncratic meanings and patterns learned within the family. Many schizophrenic patients have had little childhood peer group experience. The problem is circular, for aberrant ways of relating and communicating learned within the family create difficulties in fitting in with other children.

SUMMARY

In discussing that cardinal function of the family—the transmission of the basic adaptive techniques of the culture to the children—I have confined myself to examining the central role of language in human adaptation and the parents' role in nurturing and directing the child's linguistic abilities. Man depends upon language to transmit and assimilate the instrumentalities and institutions of the culture which he requires for adaptation, and in a scientifically oriented and rapidly changing society, he is particularly dependent upon learning useful and valid meanings to enable him to be adaptable to new conditions. The ability to control and channel basic drives, to understand the self and direct the self toward future goals, and, indeed, ego functioning in general are inherently related to the acquisition of a language and the categorization of experiences through words. Various ways in which parents impede language development, foster distrust of the utility of verbal communication, and inculcate confused or distorted meanings have been discussed. In the process, I have sought to provide a foundation for relating the personality difficulties of parents and the deficiencies of the family environment they create to the proclivity of schizophrenic offspring to distort meanings, conceptualize poorly, and to suffer ego fragmentation.

References

Aeschylus. *The Euminides.*

Alanen, Y. O. (1958). The Mothers of Schizophrenic Patients. *Acta Psychiat. Neurol. Scandinav., Suppl. 124.*

Bacon, F. (1955). The Great Instauration. In *Selected Writings of Francis Bacon.* New York: Modern Library.

Bateson, G. (1960). Minimal Requirements for a Theory of Schizophrenia. *AMA Arch. Gen. Psychiat., 2*:477-491.

Bateson, G., Jackson, D., et al. (1956). Towards a Theory of Schizophrenia. *Behavioral Sci., 1*:251-264.

Bott, E. (1957). *Family and Social Network.* London: Tavistock Publications.

Brown, R. (1958). *Words and Things.* Glencoe, Ill.: Free Press.

Bruch, H. (1961). Transformation of Oral Impulses in Eating Disorders. *Psychiat. Quart., 35*:458-481.

Bruch, H. and Palombo, S. (1961). Conceptual Problems in Schizophrenia. *J. Nerv. Ment. Dis., 132*:114-117.

Bruner, J., Goodnow, J., and Austin, G. (1956). *A Study of Thinking.* New York: J. Wiley & Sons.

Butler, S. (1927). *Erewhon.* New York: Modern Library.

Cameron, N. (1938). *Reasoning, Regression and Communication in Schizophrenics.* Psychol. Monogr., No. 221.

Dewey, J. (1925). *Experience and Nature*. London: Open Court Publishing Co.

Dewey, J. (1929). *The Quest for Certainty*. New York: Milton Balch & Co.

Doi, L. T. (1962). Amae—A Key Concept for Understanding Japanese Personality Structure. *Psychologia., 5*:1-7.

Engel, F. (1902). *The Origin of the Family, Private Property and the State*. Chicago: C. H. Kerr & Co.

Fleck, S., Lidz, T., et al. (1963). Comparison of the Parent-Child Relationships of Male and Female Schizophrenic Patients. *Arch. Gen. Psychiat., 8*:1-7.

Fleck, S., Lidz, T., et al. (1957). The Intrafamilial Environment of the Schizophrenic Patient: Incestuous and Homosexual Problems. In *Individual and Familial Dynamics,* Ed., J. Masserman. New York: Grune & Stratton.

Flugel, J. D. (1921). *The Psychoanalytic Study of the Family*. London: Hogarth Press.

Freud, S. (1913). Totem and taboo. In *The Standard Edition of the Complete Psychological Works of Sigmund Freud,* Vol. 13. London: Hogarth Press, 1955.

Freud, S. (1923). The Ego and the Id. In *The Standard Edition of the Complete Psychological Works of Sigmund Freud,* Vol. 19. London: Hogarth Press, 1961.

Hampson, J. G. (1955). Hermaphroditic Genital Appearance, Rearing and Eroticism in Hyperadrenocorticism. *Bull. Johns Hopkins Hosp., 96*:265-273.

Hampson, J. L., Hampson, J. G., et al. (1955). The Syndrome of Gonadal Agenesis (Ovarian Agenesis) and Male Chromosomal Pattern in Girls and

Women: Psychologic studies. *Bull. Johns Hopkins Hosp., 97*:207-226.

Hartmann, H. (1958). *Ego Psychology and the Problem of Adaptation.* New York: International Universities Press.

Heidegger, M. (1929). *Sein und Zeit.* Halle: M. Niemeyer.

Inhelder, B. and Piaget, J. (1958). *The Growth of Logical Thinking from Childhood to Adolescence.* New York: Basic Books.

Lidz, R. W. and Lidz, T. (1952). Therapeutic Considerations Arising from the Intense Symbiotic Needs of Schizophrenic Patients. In *Psychotherapy with Schizophrenics,* Ed., E. Brody and F. Redlich. New York: International Universities Press.

Lidz, T. (1958). Schizophrenia and the Family. *Psychiatry, 21*:21-27.

Lidz, T., Cornelison, A., et al. (1957a). The Intrafamilial Environment of the Schizophrenic Patient: I. The Father. *Psychiatry, 20*:329-342.

Lidz, T., Cornelison, A., et al. (1957b). The Intrafamilial Environment of the Schizophrenic Patient: II. Marital Schism and Marital Skew. *Am. J. Psychiat., 114*:241-248.

Lidz, T., Cornelison, A., et al. (1958a). The Intrafamilial Environment of the Schizophrenic Patient: IV. Parental Personalities and Family Interaction. *Am. J. Orthopsychiat., 28*:764-776.

Lidz, T., Cornelison, A., et al. (1958b). The Intrafamilial Environment of the Schizophrenic Patient: VI. The Transmission of Irrationality. *Arch. Neurol. Psychiat., 79*:305-316.

Lidz, T. and Fleck, S. (1960). Schizophrenia, Human Integration and the Role of the Family. In *Etiol-*

ogy of Schizophrenia, Ed., D. Jackson. New York: Basic Books.

Lidz, T., Wild, C., et al. (1962). Thought Disorders in the Parents of Schizophrenic Patients: A Study Utilizing the Object Sorting Test. *Psychiat. Research, 1*:193-200.

McCarthy, D. (1930). *The Language Development of the Pre-School Child.* Minneapolis, Minn.: University of Minnesota Press.

Mark, H. (1962). Elementary Thinking and the Classification of Behavior. *Science, 135*:75-78.

Mills, T. (1953). Power Relations in Three-Person Groups. *Am. Sociol. Rev., 18*:351-357.

Parsons, T. (1954). The Incest Taboo in Relation to Social Structure and the Socialization of the Child. *Brit. J. Sociol., 5*:101-117.

Parsons, T. and Bales, R., Eds. (1955). *Family, Socialization and Interaction Process.* Glencoe, Ill.: Free Press.

Parsons, T., Bales, R., and Shils, E., Eds. (1953). *Working Papers in the Theory of Action.* Glencoe, Ill.: Free Press.

Piaget, J. (1926). *The Language and Thought of the Child.* New York: Harcourt, Brace & Co.

Piaget, J. (1928). *Judgment and Reasoning in the Child.* New York: Harcourt, Brace & Co.

Sapir, E. (1949). *Selected Writings of Edward Sapir in Language, Culture and Personality.* Berkeley, Calif.: University of California Press.

Schafer, R., and Glaser, G. (1963). *EEG and Behavior.* New York: Basic Books.

Schevill, F. (1936). *History of Florence from the Founding of the City Through the Renaissance.* New York: Harcourt, Brace & Co.

REFERENCES

Singer, M. T. Studies in progress.

Spiegel, J. (1957). The Resolution of Role Conflict within the Family. *Psychiatry, 20*:1-16.

Spiegel, J. and Bell, N. (1959). The Family of the Psychiatric Patient. In *American Handbook of Psychiatry*, Ed., S. Arieti. New York: Basic Books.

Spiegel, J., Kluckhohn, F., et al. (1954). *Integration and Conflict in Family Behavior.* Topeka, Kansas: Group for the Advancement of Psychiatry, Report 27.

Strodtbeck, F. (1954). The Family as a Three-Person Group. *Am. Sociol. Rev., 19*:23-29.

Timasheff, N. (1946). *The Great Retreat.* New York: E. P. Dutton.

Vygotsky, L. S. (1934). Thought in Schizophrenia. *Arch. Neurol. Psychiat., 31*:1063-1077.

Vygotsky, L. S. (1962). *Thought and Language.* New York: J. Wiley & Sons and M.I.T. Press.

Weakland, J. (1960). The "Double-Bind" Hypothesis of Schizophrenia and Three-Party Interaction. In *Etiology of Schizophrenia*, Ed., D. Jackson. New York: Basic Books.

Whorf, B. (1940). Science and Linguistics. *Technol. Rev., 42*:229-231, 247-248.

Whorf, B. (1941a). Languages and Logic. *Technol. Rev., 43*:250-252, 266, 268, 272.

Whorf, B. (1941b). The Relation of Habitual Thought and Behavior to Language. In *Language, Culture and Personality*, Ed., L. Spier. Menasha, Wisconsin: Sapir Memorial Publication Fund.

Whorf, B. (1942). Language, Mind, and Reality. *Theosophist, 63*(1):281-291, (2)25-37.

Whorf, B. (1956). *Language, Thought, and Reality. Selected Writings of Benjamin Lee Whorf.* Ed., J.

Carroll. New York: M.I.T. and J. Wiley & Sons.

Wynne, L. C., Ryckoff, I., et al. (1958). Pseudo-Mutuality in the Family Relations of Schizophrenics. *Psychiatry, 21*:205-220.

Zimmerman, C. (1947). *Family and Civilization.* New York: Harper Bros.